Navigating Leadership: Steer with Vision

From Understanding Team Dynamics to Harnessing Personal Strengths: A Comprehensive Guide for Aspiring Leaders

Alexander Thornton

Summary

Chapter 1: Introduction to Leadership Dynamics

Leadership is an intricate and multifaceted concept that has intrigued scholars, practitioners, and individuals for centuries. From ancient civilizations to modern-day organizations, the idea of leadership and its dynamics have evolved as societies have progressed. In this chapter, we will embark on a transformative journey exploring the foundational principles and dynamics that underpin effective leadership. We will delve into different leadership styles, examine the key attributes of successful leaders, and analyze the delicate balance between leadership and followership.

The Essence of Leadership

Leadership constitutes the ability to influence, inspire, and guide individuals towards a common goal. It serves as the catalyst for positive change, empowering people to exceed their own expectations and accomplish remarkable feats. Whether in a business, political, or social context, successful leaders possess a unique combination of skills, knowledge, and personal traits that enable them to motivate and mobilize others. By understanding the essence of leadership, we can unlock our untapped potential and enhance our ability to make a meaningful impact on those around us.

Leadership Styles

Leadership styles play a critical role in shaping the overall dynamics within a team or organization. Different circumstances may necessitate the adoption of various leadership styles to effectively address the challenges at hand. There are several prominent leadership styles, each with its strengths and weaknesses. Autocratic leadership, for example, involves a leader making decisions independently, relying heavily on their authority. While this style can lead to quick decision-making and efficient operations, it may stifle creativity and discourage employee engagement.

On the other hand, democratic leadership fosters a participatory and inclusive environment, involving team members in the decision-making process. This style encourages collaboration, innovation, and ensures buy-in from employees. However, it requires strong alignment in values and objectives, as it can sometimes result in prolonged decision-making due to the consensus-building nature of this style. In addition, laissez-faire leadership empowers team members to take ownership of their work, nurturing a sense of autonomy and self-direction. Although this style encourages independent thinking, it may lead to a lack of structure and diluted accountability.

Successful Leaders

Exceptional leaders possess a myriad of attributes that enable them to inspire and lead others effectively. They exhibit exceptional communication skills, allowing them to articulate a compelling vision, build relationships, and provide constructive feedback. By actively listening and empathizing, leaders create an environment that fosters trust and openness. Moreover, successful leaders demonstrate resilience, adaptability, and an aptitude for critical thinking. They have a strong sense of self-awareness, recognize their strengths and weaknesses, and surround themselves with individuals who complement their skills.

Furthermore, effective leaders display a genuine passion for lifelong learning. They seek out new experiences, explore diverse perspectives, and continuously develop their knowledge and skills. To motivate their teams, they cultivate a positive and supportive atmosphere, celebrating achievements, and recognizing effort. As a result, successful leaders create a sense of belonging and purpose, empowering their followers to consistently exceed expectations.

The Interplay of Leadership and Followership

Leadership is not a one-sided endeavor; it is closely intertwined with followership. The relationship between leaders and their followers is symbiotic. Effective leadership inspires and empowers individuals, while dedicated followers provide essential support and contribute to the achievement of shared objectives. Both leaders and followers impact and influence each other, shaping the overall dynamics within the team or organization.

Followers who exhibit active engagement, trust, and commitment contribute to building a high-performance culture. Conversely, leaders who recognize and value their followers' contributions create a sense of belonging and purpose, nurturing mutual respect and collaboration. This reciprocal relationship fosters a positive work environment, fostering innovation, productivity, and growth.

Chapter 1: to Leadership Dynamics has explored the fundamental concepts and dynamics that underpin effective leadership. From understanding the essence of leadership to examining different leadership styles and attributes, we have begun to unravel the intricate nature of leadership. Furthermore, we have discussed the symbiotic relationship between leadership and followership, highlighting the significance of collaboration and mutual respect. As we continue our journey through subsequent chapters, we will delve deeper into various aspects of leadership dynamics, such as emotional intelligence, transformational leadership, and ethical decision-making. By expanding our knowledge of leadership and its dynamics, we will acquire the tools necessary to cultivate our own leadership potential and foster a positive impact on those around us. Remember, leadership is not defined solely by a title or position; true leadership is an attitude and a state of mind that inspires others to reach new heights.

Understanding the Essence of Leadership

Leadership has long been an enigmatic concept that has captivated the minds of scholars, philosophers, and practitioners alike. It is a trait that has propelled nations to greatness, inspired social change, and transformed organizations into thriving entities. But what exactly is the essence of leadership? Is it an inherent quality possessed by a select few, or can it be nurtured and developed by anyone willing to embark on the journey of becoming a leader?

In this chapter, we shall delve deep into the intricacies of leadership, deciphering its essence and shedding light on its fundamental elements. Through exploring various theories and examples of leadership, we seek to gain a better understanding of this dynamic and multifaceted phenomenon.

The Many Faces of Leadership:

Leadership, as a concept, is not restricted solely to those occupying high-ranking positions or formal titles. In fact, leadership can be observed at all levels and in various domains, from grassroots community leaders to influential social activists to inspiring mentors. Leadership is not defined by a title, but by the ability to influence, inspire, and guide others to achieve a common purpose.

Different Theories, One Essence:

Numerous theories have been proposed to understand leadership, each offering a unique perspective on its essence. The trait theory emphasizes that certain inherent qualities, such as intelligence, confidence, and charisma, are vital for effective leadership. According to this theory, leaders possess a set of traits that distinguish them from followers, making them more suited for leadership roles.

On the other hand, the behavioral theory argues that leadership is not solely reliant on inherent traits, but rather on observable behaviors. Leaders who exhibit task-oriented behaviors focus on achieving goals and maintaining productivity, while those with relationship-oriented behaviors prioritize building strong interpersonal relationships within the team.

Moving beyond individual traits and behaviors, the situational theory posits that effective leadership is contingent upon the situation and context in which it occurs. It suggests that leaders must adapt their approach based on the needs of their followers and the demands of the situation. This flexibility enables leaders to respond appropriately to different challenges and maximize their impact.

Diving deeper into the essence of leadership, the transformational theory suggests that true leaders go beyond merely managing tasks or inspiring followers. They have the remarkable ability to inspire, motivate, and transform individuals and organizations, challenging the status quo and bringing about positive change.

Elements of Effective Leadership:

While theories help us understand different facets of leadership, there are certain core elements that underpin its essence. These elements, when cultivated and harnessed, can help aspiring leaders carve their path towards effectiveness and influence.

1. Vision and Purpose: Leadership begins with a compelling vision and a clear sense of purpose. Effective leaders have the ability to envision a better future and articulate their goals, inspiring others to align their efforts towards a shared vision.

2. Emotional Intelligence: Understanding emotions, both within oneself and others, is crucial for effective leadership. Leaders with high emotional intelligence can empathize with their followers, connect on a deeper level, and build trust, fostering an environment conducive to growth and collaboration.

3. Communication Skills: Communication lies at the heart of leadership. Leaders must be able to articulate their thoughts clearly, listen actively, and adapt their communication style to resonate with different individuals and audiences. Effective communication helps

foster understanding, inspires action, and enables collaboration.

4. Integrity and Ethics: Exceptional leaders uphold high ethical standards and demonstrate integrity in their actions. By leading with authenticity, honesty, and transparency, they inspire trust and create a culture of accountability and ethical behavior within their team.

5. Adaptability and Resilience: In an ever-changing world, adaptability is crucial for leaders to thrive. Effective leaders embrace change, remain agile in the face of uncertainty, and learn from failures. Through resilience, they inspire their followers to persevere and navigate challenges with a positive mindset.

6. Empowerment and Development: Leaders recognize the potential in their team members and strive to empower them to reach their full potential. By investing in their development, providing guidance, and fostering a supportive environment, leaders create a legacy of growth and success.

While this chapter offers an exploration into the essence of leadership, it only scratches the surface of this vast and evolving field. Leadership is both an art and a science, constantly shaped by societal dynamics and individual aspirations. Through understanding its various theories and core elements, individuals can embark upon their own journey of leadership, continuously learning, growing, and inspiring others.

Remember, leadership is not a destination but a lifelong pursuit, with personal growth and impact as its ultimate rewards.

Defining Leadership Styles

Leadership is a complex phenomenon that permeates every aspect of human existence. From politics to business, education to sports, effective leadership is essential for both personal and collective success. Just as there are different types of leaders, there are various styles of leadership that individuals employ to influence and guide others towards a common goal. In this chapter, we will delve into the diverse landscape of leadership styles, exploring their characteristics, strengths, and weaknesses.

The Concept of Leadership Styles

Before we delve into the specifics, let us first establish a comprehensive understanding of what leadership styles are. A leadership style refers to a leader's approach in terms of how they interact with and influence their team members or followers. It encompasses a leader's behaviors, attitudes, and values, which when combined, form unique patterns that define their leadership style. Leadership styles are not static; they can be developed, refined, and adapted to various situations and contexts.

Autocratic Leadership Style

Autocratic leadership is characterized by its hierarchical structure, where the leader makes decisions independently without seeking input or considering the opinions of others. The autocratic leader expects strict adherence to their instructions and rarely delegates any authority to subordinates. While this leadership style may appear domineering, it can be effective in situations requiring quick decision-making or in highly structured environments.

One of the main advantages of autocratic leadership is its ability to maintain control and direction. With a clear chain of command, decisions can be implemented swiftly, enabling productivity and goal attainment. However, this style may foster an environment of dependency and hinder creativity and innovation due to the lack of involvement from team members.

Authoritative Leadership Style

Contrary to the autocratic leadership style, the authoritative leadership style emphasizes collaboration and open communication. An authoritative leader provides clear direction and establishes goals while involving team members in decision-making processes. They encourage feedback, value divergent opinions, and empower subordinates to take ownership of their work.

This leadership style thrives in situations that require a visionary perspective. By fostering a culture of trust and transparency, the authoritative leader inspires commitment and engagement from team members. However, this style may become ineffective when leaders fail to establish a clear vision or without the ability to effectively communicate their expectations.

Democratic Leadership Style

Often hailed as the epitome of participatory leadership, the democratic style emphasizes inclusivity, shared decision-making, and consensus-building. Democratic leaders collaborate with team members, encouraging them to voice their opinions, share ideas, and actively participate in shaping organizational goals and strategies.

The democratic style values input from various stakeholders, fostering a sense of ownership and enthusiasm amongst team members. This approach can lead to increased motivation, creativity, and a higher level of job satisfaction. However, decision-making processes can be time-consuming, and disagreements may arise, thus requiring effective conflict resolution skills from the leader.

Laissez-Faire Leadership Style

Derived from the French phrase meaning "let them do," the laissez-faire leadership style involves minimal interference from the leader. Leaders utilizing this style grant significant autonomy to their team members, allowing them to make decisions and complete tasks with little to no guidance or supervision.

This leadership style is suitable for highly skilled and self-motivated individuals who require minimal direction. It promotes personal growth, encourages innovative thinking, and leads to increased job satisfaction. However, in the absence of clear expectations or feedback, team members may experience confusion and lack of guidance, resulting in a decline in productivity and accountability.

Transactional Leadership Style

Transactional leadership operates on the principle of reward and punishment. Leaders utilizing this style establish clear expectations, goals, and performance criteria for their team members. They maintain a transactional relationship by providing rewards or recognition for achieving desired outcomes and offering corrective measures or consequences for failing to meet expectations.

This leadership style establishes clear accountability and fosters a results-oriented culture. The transactional leader motivates through extrinsic rewards, such as bonuses or promotions, and successfully drives performance. However, the over-reliance on rewards and punishments may hinder intrinsic motivation, limit creativity, and stifle innovation.

Transformational Leadership Style

Contrasting with the transactional style, the transformational leadership style focuses on empowering and inspiring followers to transcend their self-interests and work towards a collective purpose. Transformational leaders lead by example, cultivating trust, vision, and passion within their teams.

These leaders exhibit charisma and display high levels of emotional intelligence. By fostering open communication, providing mentorship, and recognizing individual growth, transformational leaders build strong relationships with their teams. They inspire enthusiasm, creativity, and a shared commitment towards achieving organizational goals. However, the transformational style may have limitations when more immediate and specific guidance is required.

Servant Leadership Style

Servant leadership stands out for its emphasis on the well-being and development of followers. Servant leaders prioritize the growth and success of their team members, acting as mentors and facilitators. They aim to serve others before themselves, focusing on nurturing a positive and supportive work environment.

By placing the needs of their followers first, servant leaders build strong foundations of trust, loyalty, and collaboration. This approach fosters commitment, satisfaction, and personal growth among team members. However, servant leadership may become problematic in situations where decisive action or firm direction is necessary, requiring adaptability and flexibility from the leader.

Leadership styles are multidimensional and fluid in nature. Effective leaders possess the ability to adapt their style based on the context, goals, and needs of their team members. While each leadership style holds its own strengths and weaknesses, understanding and leveraging a diverse range of styles can contribute to effective leadership and successful team outcomes.

By embracing a comprehensive understanding of leadership styles and recognizing their nuances, leaders can cultivate and refine their own approach to bring out the best in themselves and those they lead. The exploration and mastery of leadership styles are an ongoing journey, with continuous learning and improvement as the ultimate goal.

Importance of Effective Leadership in Today's World

In the rapidly evolving landscape of the 21st century, leadership has emerged as a critical factor in achieving success in various spheres of life, be it in businesses, politics, education, or other domains. The importance of effective leadership cannot be overstated, as it sets the tone for organizations, shapes societies, and inspires individuals to reach their fullest potential. In this chapter, we will delve into the multifaceted dimensions of leadership and explore how it exerts a profound influence on today's world.

The Changing Dynamics of Leadership:

Gone are the days when leaders were revered simply for their authoritative power or position. Today, leadership is not about ruling from a distance but is centered on building relationships, fostering collaboration, and empowering others. The approach to leadership has transitioned from a hierarchical control structure to one that emphasizes inclusivity, empathy, and adaptability.

1. Inspiring Trust and Vision:

At the core of effective leadership lies the ability to inspire trust and vision. Leaders who can articulate a compelling vision that resonates with their followers can ignite passion, motivation, and a collective drive towards a common goal. Moreover, leaders who model transparency, integrity, and ethical conduct cultivate trust and credibility, allowing them to influence their teams more effectively.

2. Nurturing Emotional Intelligence:

Leadership is not merely about setting goals or making executive decisions; it is about understanding and engaging with people at an emotional level. Emotional intelligence — the ability to recognize, understand, and manage emotions in oneself and others — empowers leaders to be more attuned to the needs, concerns, and aspirations of their team members. By fostering emotional connection and empathy, leaders can create a positive work environment that fosters collaboration, creativity, and loyalty.

3. Embracing Diversity and Inclusion:

In today's diverse and interconnected world, effective leadership demands an appreciation for the power of diversity. Leaders who cultivate an inclusive culture by valuing different perspectives, backgrounds, and experiences create an environment that fosters innovation, creativity, and adaptability. They recognize that diverse teams are more likely to generate groundbreaking ideas and solutions.

Leadership in Different Domains:

Leadership is not restricted to the corporate realm; it extends into various domains, each with its unique challenges and opportunities. Let's explore the importance of effective leadership in different fields:

1. Business and Entrepreneurship:

In the fiercely competitive world of business, effective leadership is a differentiating factor that determines whether a company thrives or flounders. Business leaders play a pivotal role in formulating strategies, championing innovation, cultivating a customer-centric mindset, and fostering a culture of continuous learning and growth. The success of an organization often hinges on the ability of its leaders to adapt to change, anticipate market trends, and guide their teams towards excellence.

2. Politics and Governance:

In the realm of politics and governance, effective leadership can shape the destiny of nations and influence the lives of millions. Skillful politicians leverage their charisma, communication prowess, and ability to inspire trust to rally support, forge coalitions, and implement transformative policies. Leadership in politics necessitates a firm commitment to ethical governance, public service, and the well-being of constituents.

3. Education and Academia:

The role of leadership in education is instrumental in shaping not only the minds of individuals but also the future of societies. Educational leaders set the vision for institutions, drive educational reforms, and create learning environments that foster critical thinking, creativity, and lifelong learning. Effective leaders in academia empower teachers, students, and parents to collaborate towards a shared educational goal, ensuring the holistic development of future generations.

4. Social and Nonprofit Organizations:

Leadership in social and nonprofit organizations involves navigating complex social challenges and working towards creating a positive impact on a local, national, or global scale. Effective leaders in these sectors possess a deep sense of empathy, social consciousness, and a commitment to social justice. They mobilize resources, galvanize volunteers, and inspire collective action to address pressing issues such as poverty, inequality, and environmental degradation.

The Challenges of Leadership:

While the significance of effective leadership is crystal clear, the path to becoming a successful leader is neither straightforward nor without challenges. Leaders face a myriad of hurdles, both internal and external, that test their mettle and resilience. Some common challenges include:

1. Adapting to Change:

Leaders are constantly confronted with change that can come from technological advancements, evolving consumer preferences, global disruptions, or internal restructuring. Effective leaders must possess the agility to adapt to these shifts, anticipate their impact, and guide their teams through periods of uncertainty. The ability to navigate change not only ensures organizational survival but also fosters a culture of resilience, learning, and growth.

2. Overcoming Resistance:

Leadership often involves challenging the status quo and implementing changes that may be met with resistance or pushback. Effective leaders must demonstrate persuasive communication skills to articulate the need for change, address concerns, and build consensus. The art of navigating resistance requires empathy, active listening, and a willingness to incorporate diverse perspectives.

3. Building and Sustaining High-Performing Teams:

Leadership is not a solitary endeavor but an opportunity to inspire and guide a team towards shared objectives. Building and sustaining high-performing teams necessitate effective communication, delegation, and a focus on cultivating a culture of collaboration, trust, and accountability. Moreover, leaders must be adept at recognizing and nurturing the strengths of individuals within the team, encouraging diversity of viewpoints and fostering an environment conducive to innovation and growth.

Effective leadership has never been more crucial than in today's dynamic, interconnected world. Whether in businesses, politics, education, or nonprofit organizations, leaders play a pivotal role in shaping the present and future. By cultivating emotional intelligence, embracing diversity, and inspiring trust and vision, leaders can create transformative change, unlock the potential of individuals and organizations, and contribute to a better world.

Leadership is a lifelong journey, constantly evolving to address the unique challenges of each era. Successful leaders are those who continue to learn, adapt, and grow, all while staying true to their core values. As we navigate the complexities of the 21st century, the importance of effective leadership will continue to shape our collective destiny, laying the foundations for a more prosperous, inclusive, and sustainable world.

Challenges Faced by Aspiring Leaders

Leadership is a journey that is filled with numerous challenges and obstacles. It requires dedication, perseverance, and resilience to overcome the hurdles that come in the way of aspiring leaders. In this chapter, we delve into the unique challenges faced by those who aspire to lead, offering insights and guidance on how to navigate these difficulties with grace and success. Through understanding and addressing these challenges, aspiring leaders can develop the necessary skills and qualities to thrive in their leadership roles.

The Loneliness of Leadership:

One of the first challenges aspiring leaders encounter is the sense of isolation and loneliness that often accompanies leadership positions. As responsibilities increase, leaders may find themselves distanced from their peers and colleagues, unable to fully share their experiences and concerns. The weight of decision-making can become overwhelming, making it necessary for aspiring leaders to leverage support networks – both within and outside their organization – to combat this sense of isolation. Developing strong relationships with mentors, seeking counsel from experienced leaders, and joining professional networks can all help alleviate the loneliness that aspiring leaders commonly face.

Embracing Uncertainty:

Leadership is often synonymous with uncertainty. Aspiring leaders

must step into the unknown, making decisions and taking actions
that do not come with guarantees. This degree of ambiguity can be
distressing for many, as they navigate uncharted territories and face
difficult choices. Embracing uncertainty is a pivotal challenge that
aspiring leaders must conquer by developing adaptability and
resilience. Cultivating a growth mindset, seeking feedback, and
encouraging experimentation within their teams are strategies that
can help aspiring leaders become comfortable with uncertainty and
turn it into an opportunity for growth and innovation.

Leading Through Change:

Change is a constant in the world of leadership, and aspiring leaders
must be adept at leading their teams through periods of transition.
Change can be met with resistance and fear, making it a challenging
task for aspiring leaders to inspire and motivate others during these
times. The ability to communicate the benefits of change effectively,
creating a shared vision, and fostering a culture of openness and
trust are essential qualities for aspiring leaders to effectively
navigate change. By instilling confidence in their teams and leading
by example, aspiring leaders can successfully guide their
organizations towards a better future.

Managing Conflict:

Conflict is an inherent part of any leadership position. Aspiring
leaders need to develop the skills to address and manage conflicts
constructively and proactively. Conflict may arise due to differences

in opinions, personalities, or values within a team. Successful aspiring leaders are adept at facilitating open dialogue, active listening, and finding mutually beneficial solutions. By creating a safe environment for healthy debate and promoting conflict resolution strategies, leaders can turn conflicts into opportunities for growth and collaboration.

Navigating Politics:

Leadership, especially in organizational settings, often entails navigating complex political landscapes. Aspiring leaders may find themselves dealing with competing interests, power struggles, and office politics. Developing political acumen is crucial for aspiring leaders to understand the dynamics at play and make informed decisions. It requires building solid relationships, maintaining neutrality, and being skilled in negotiation and compromise. By navigating politics with integrity and transparency, aspiring leaders can establish trust and credibility among their team members while achieving their organizational goals.

Building and Empowering a Team:

Aspiring leaders must recognize that their success is directly tied to the success of their team. Building and empowering a high-performing team can be a daunting challenge. The leader's ability to recruit diverse talent, foster collaboration, and provide opportunities for growth and development are key factors in team success. Aspiring leaders need to invest time and effort into understanding their team members' strengths, offering support, and creating a culture of empowerment. By fostering a sense of ownership and accountability within the team, aspiring leaders can drive their organization towards excellence.

Balancing Personal and Professional Life:

Leadership demands significant time and energy, often blurring the lines between personal and professional life. Aspiring leaders must grapple with the challenge of maintaining a healthy work-life balance while pursuing their career aspirations. This balance requires setting boundaries, prioritizing self-care, and leveraging support systems. Aspiring leaders must recognize that their well-being is vital to their effectiveness as leaders, and they should strive to create a harmonious integration of personal and professional life.

In this chapter, we have explored the challenges faced by aspiring leaders as they journey towards leadership roles. The loneliness of leadership, embracing uncertainty, leading through change, managing conflict, navigating politics, building and empowering a team, and balancing personal and professional life are all critical challenges aspiring leaders must tackle. By recognizing and addressing these challenges head-on, aspiring leaders can develop the skills, qualities, and resilience necessary to excel in leadership positions. This chapter serves as a guide, providing aspiring leaders with insights and strategies to overcome these hurdles and emerge as effective and respected leaders.

Chapter 2: Grasping Team Dynamics

In any successful endeavor, be it in business, sports, or any other field, the ability to work effectively in a team is a crucial component. Team dynamics play a pivotal role in determining the success or failure of a team's objectives. Understanding and mastering team dynamics is an invaluable skill that can greatly enhance one's personal and professional life. This chapter aims to delve deep into the intricacies of team dynamics, exploring various aspects such as team formation, roles and responsibilities, communication, conflict resolution, and cohesion. By grasping these fundamental concepts, individuals can unlock the true potential of their teams and achieve remarkable outcomes.

Section 1: The Formation of a Team

Forming a team is often the starting point of any group endeavor. However, the composition and formation process of a team are critical factors that can impact its effectiveness. Building a well-balanced team involves considering various aspects, such as individuals' skills, experiences, and personalities. When assembling a team, it is essential to seek diversity in perspectives and skill sets to foster creativity and innovation. Moreover, paying attention to team size and member roles is crucial in harnessing the collective abilities of the team.

Section 2: Roles and Responsibilities

One key factor in successful team dynamics lies in clearly defining roles and responsibilities within the team. Each team member should understand their specific responsibilities and how they contribute to the team's overall objectives. This section emphasizes the importance of effective delegation, ensuring that tasks are assigned to individuals based on their strengths and expertise. Additionally, encouraging team members to take ownership of their roles and fostering a spirit of accountability is vital to achieving high-performance levels.

Section 3: Effective Communication

Communication is the lifeblood of any team, and it plays a pivotal role in team dynamics. This section explores the various aspects of effective communication within a team, including active listening, clarity of expression, and open and honest dialogue. It highlights the significance of fostering a safe and non-judgmental environment where team members feel comfortable expressing their thoughts and ideas. Effective communication not only ensures that everyone is on the same page but also fosters trust and collaboration among team members.

Section 4: Conflict Resolution

In any team, conflicts and disagreements are inevitable due to differences in opinions, perspectives, and working styles. However, conflicts, if managed effectively, can lead to innovation and growth.

This section delves into the importance of embracing and resolving conflicts in a productive manner. It provides guidance on strategies for constructive conflict resolution, such as active listening, seeking common ground, and encouraging compromise. By addressing conflicts head-on and promoting a culture of understanding and respect, teams can overcome obstacles and strengthen their dynamics.

Section 5: Building Team Cohesion

Cohesion, the sense of unity and collaboration within a team, is a vital ingredient for success. In this section, readers explore various methods to build and maintain team cohesion, such as team-building activities, fostering a supportive culture, and recognizing and celebrating achievements. It emphasizes the significance of nurturing a positive team environment where trust, respect, and camaraderie flourish. By instilling a sense of belonging and shared purpose, team cohesion can create a strong foundation for achieving outstanding results.

Section 6: Monitoring and Adapting

The dynamics within a team are not fixed; they evolve over time. This section explores the importance of regularly monitoring team dynamics and adapting strategies accordingly. It highlights the significance of feedback loops, both formal and informal, to gauge team performance and address any emerging issues promptly. Additionally, it encourages leaders and team members to be open to change and continuously seek opportunities for growth and improvement.

Understanding and mastering team dynamics is an ongoing journey that requires constant effort and commitment. By recognizing the complexities of team formation, clarifying roles and responsibilities, fostering effective communication, embracing conflicts, building cohesion, and monitoring progress, teams can unlock their full potential. By implementing the insights provided in this chapter, individuals can develop strong team dynamics that propel them towards unprecedented success. Whether you are leading a team or contributing as a member, grasping team dynamics will undoubtedly provide you with a significant competitive advantage and enrich your personal and professional life.

Forming Successful Teams

In today's fast-paced and highly competitive world, teams have become the backbone of organizations. Whether it's a small startup or a multinational corporation, teams play a vital role in achieving success. However, forming successful teams is no easy task. It requires careful planning, effective communication, and a deep understanding of human dynamics. In this chapter, we will explore the key elements and strategies for forming successful teams.

Understanding Team Dynamics

Before delving into the intricacies of forming successful teams, it is crucial to understand the dynamics that govern team functioning. Teams are made up of individuals with diverse skills, experiences, and personalities. The successful amalgamation of these factors contributes to a team's overall performance.

One of the fundamental aspects of team dynamics is the need for complementary skills. A team that consists of individuals with various expertise and knowledge sets can bring fresh perspectives and innovative ideas to the table. Furthermore, the diversity within the team fosters a culture of learning and growth, as members can learn from each other's strengths.

Another essential aspect is effective communication. A team that establishes open and transparent channels of communication ensures that all members are on the same page. Clear communication helps avoid misunderstandings, promotes collaboration, and facilitates quick decision-making.

The Stages of Team Formation

For teams to function optimally, it is necessary to navigate through several stages of formation. Understanding these stages can provide insights into team dynamics and guide leaders in managing their teams effectively.

1. Forming: In this initial stage, team members are introduced to one another and begin to explore their roles and responsibilities. The forming stage is characterized by uncertainty, as individuals are often unfamiliar with their team members' strengths and work styles.

2. Storming: Once the forming stage is complete, conflicts and differences of opinion may arise. This stage is critical for the team's growth as it forces members to address these conflicts openly and find common ground. Effective leadership is crucial in managing conflicts constructively to prevent them from escalating and damaging team cohesion.

3. Norming: After the storming stage, teams establish clear goals,

shared values, and norms for acceptable behavior. Norms determine the rules and expectations within the team and help foster a supportive environment. At this stage, team members start building trust and developing a sense of camaraderie.

4. Performing: When teams reach the performing stage, they showcase their true potential. Having resolved conflicts, established norms, and built trust, team members work seamlessly together towards accomplishing their goals. In this stage, individuals are motivated, collaborative, and highly productive.

Forming Effective Teams

Now that we have a solid understanding of team dynamics and the different stages of formation let's delve into the strategies and practices to form successful teams.

1. Define clear goals and roles: The foundation of a successful team lies in defining clear goals and establishing individual roles and responsibilities. When members understand their objectives and how their contributions fit into the bigger picture, it enhances their commitment and accountability.

2. Create diverse teams: As mentioned earlier, diversity within a team brings valuable perspectives and insights. Aim to build teams that encompass individuals with diverse backgrounds, skills, and

experiences. This diversity encourages creative problem-solving, fosters innovation, and broadens the team's overall capabilities.

3. Foster effective communication: Communication is the lifeline of a successful team. Encourage open and honest communication channels that allow team members to express their ideas, concerns, and feedback. Ensure that there is active listening and respect for one another's opinions. Regular team meetings, brainstorming sessions, and project update discussions can help facilitate effective communication.

4. Build trust and psychological safety: Trust is the bedrock of any successful team. Cultivate an environment where team members feel safe to take risks, make mistakes, and voice their opinions without fear of judgment. Celebrate each other's achievements and foster a supportive culture that boosts motivation and collaboration.

5. Emphasize shared values and norms: Clearly define the values and norms that govern the team's behavior. Encourage a culture of respect, integrity, and accountability. When everyone abides by the same set of rules, it creates a sense of coherence, enabling the team to handle challenges smoothly and remain focused on its objectives.

6. Encourage collaborative problem-solving: Promote a problem-solving mindset within the team. Encourage members to actively contribute ideas, seek input from others, and collaborate on finding

solutions. This not only allows for more robust decision-making but also creates a sense of ownership and commitment towards the team's goals.

Forming successful teams is an art that requires careful consideration of team dynamics, effective leadership, and continuous effort. By understanding the different stages of team formation, embracing diversity, fostering effective communication, building trust, and emphasizing shared values, organizations can create high-performing teams that drive success. Remember that forming successful teams is an ongoing process that requires regular evaluation and adaptation as the team evolves. With dedication and a focus on these strategies, any leader can build a winning team capable of conquering even the most challenging goals.

Roles and Responsibilities within Teams

In today's fast-paced and interconnected world, teamwork has become an integral part of our everyday lives. Whether it is within organizations, sports teams, or community groups, the success of a team depends on the individuals who contribute their unique skills, experiences, and perspectives. However, for teams to function effectively, it is essential to have clear roles and responsibilities for each team member. This chapter delves into the significance of roles and responsibilities within teams and explores how they contribute to team success.

Understanding Roles within a Team

When we think about a team, we envision a group of individuals working together towards a common goal. However, it is important to recognize that each team member has a distinct role to play in order to achieve that goal efficiently and effectively.

Roles refer to the specific tasks, functions, or areas of responsibility assigned to team members to ensure the smooth functioning and progress of the team. These roles are often determined by various factors, including an individual's skills, expertise, experience, and personal attributes.

Roles can be broadly classified into two categories: formal and informal roles. Formal roles are typically predetermined and assigned based on the team's requirements. These roles are often defined by job titles or specific functions such as team leader, project manager, or data analyst. Informal roles, on the other hand, emerge naturally within the team based on individuals' personalities and abilities. Examples of informal roles include the peacemaker, the motivator, or the idea generator.

While formal roles provide structure and clarity, informal roles can significantly influence team dynamics, cohesion, and performance. Both types of roles are crucial for the success of the team, and it is essential to strike a balance between them.

Defining Responsibilities within a Team

Responsibilities go hand in hand with roles within a team. They refer to the obligations, duties, or tasks that each team member is accountable for in order to fulfill their respective role and contribute to the team's objectives.

Responsibilities within a team can vary based on the nature of the team, the goals to be achieved, and the specific tasks or functions assigned to each member. However, there are some broad categories of responsibilities that are common to most teams, including:

1. Task-related Responsibilities: These responsibilities are directly

linked to the accomplishment of the team's assigned tasks or projects. They involve executing specific actions, meeting deadlines, and delivering quality outcomes. For example, a software developer in a team might be responsible for coding, debugging, and testing software applications.

2. Communication Responsibilities: Effective communication is vital for team success. Team members have a responsibility to ensure clear and open lines of communication within the team. This includes actively listening, sharing information, providing feedback, and resolving conflicts constructively. For instance, a team member might be responsible for organizing regular team meetings, ensuring everyone is informed about progress, and facilitating effective communication channels.

3. Decision-making Responsibilities: Teams often encounter situations where decisions need to be made collectively. Each team member has a responsibility to actively participate in the decision-making process by sharing their opinions, insights, and expertise. By engaging in constructive debate, teams can arrive at informed decisions that align with their goals and objectives.

4. Supportive Responsibilities: A strong sense of camaraderie and support within a team is crucial for motivation, productivity, and overall team morale. Each team member has a responsibility to support their colleagues, offer help when needed, and foster a

positive team environment. This can be as simple as lending a listening ear or providing assistance to a team member experiencing difficulties.

Team Member Dynamics and Interaction

Effective collaboration within a team requires an understanding of the dynamics and interaction patterns between team members. These dynamics influence how roles and responsibilities are perceived, accepted, and executed, ultimately affecting the team's overall performance.

1. Role Clarity: For a team to function effectively, it is essential for each team member to have a clear understanding of their role and the roles of their colleagues. Clarity helps minimize confusion, prevent duplication of efforts, and ensures that everyone knows what is expected of them. It is the responsibility of team leaders or managers to clearly communicate these roles and promote transparency within the team.

2. Role Flexibility: While roles are assigned based on individuals' skills and expertise, it is crucial to acknowledge that teams often encounter unexpected challenges or changes during the course of their work. Team members should be open to being flexible and adaptable to fulfill tasks beyond their designated roles when the situation demands. This flexibility promotes an agile team that can

respond to changing circumstances effectively.

3. Task Interdependence: In most team settings, tasks are interconnected, and the completion of one task often depends on the successful completion of others. Understanding and respecting this interdependence is vital for effective teamwork. Each team member must be aware of how their responsibilities relate to the broader goals and how their actions impact the progress of others. Recognizing the value of each team member's contribution fosters a sense of collaboration and interconnectedness.

4. Effective Communication: Collaboration within a team heavily relies on effective communication. Team members should actively listen, express their thoughts clearly, and provide constructive feedback. Strong communication helps in avoiding misunderstandings, resolving conflicts, and ensuring that everyone is on the same page. Furthermore, it allows for insights and ideas to be shared, leading to more innovative and comprehensive solutions to challenges.

Roles and responsibilities are the foundation of successful teamwork. The clear definition of roles allows individuals to understand their areas of contribution and expertise, fostering a sense of ownership and accountability. Likewise, well-defined responsibilities ensure that each team member understands their tasks and expectations, enabling effective planning and execution of team goals.

Communication Strategies for Leadership

In today's fast-paced and complex world, effective communication is crucial for leaders to foster synergy, build trust, and achieve organizational goals. Exceptional leaders understand that communication is not just about exchanging messages but also about connecting, motivating, and inspiring their teams. They have mastered various communication strategies that allow them to transmit their vision, values, and expectations effectively. This chapter will explore some key communication strategies for leadership and provide insights into how leaders can employ them to navigate through the challenges of the modern workplace.

Clear and Engaging Communication

One of the most fundamental aspects of effective leadership communication is clarity. Leaders must be able to articulate their ideas, goals, and expectations in a way that is easily understood by their teams. Clarity eliminates ambiguity and ensures that everyone is on the same page. To enhance clarity, leaders should use simple and concise language while avoiding jargon or technical terms that may confuse their audience.

In addition to clarity, engaging communication is crucial for leaders to capture and maintain the attention of their teams. Engaging communication involves conveying information in a dynamic and captivating manner that sparks interest and encourages active participation. Leaders can achieve this by using storytelling techniques, incorporating humor, and using visuals to support their messages.

Active Listening

Effective communication is a two-way process. Leaders must not only be excellent speakers but also adept listeners. Active listening is a powerful communication strategy that allows leaders to understand their team members, address their concerns, and build strong relationships.

To practice active listening, leaders must set aside distractions and give their complete attention to the speaker. They must avoid interrupting and show empathy through non-verbal cues such as nodding, maintaining eye contact, and providing feedback. Active listening fosters an environment of trust and openness, enabling leaders to gain valuable insights, make informed decisions, and address issues promptly.

Empowerment through Feedback

Feedback plays a vital role in enhancing communication effectiveness and promoting continuous improvement. Effective leaders provide constructive feedback to their teams regularly, acknowledging their achievements and identifying areas for growth.

To ensure feedback is effective, leaders should provide specific and actionable suggestions. They should focus on behavior rather than personal traits, ensuring that their feedback is objective and promotes learning. Additionally, leaders must create a safe and non-judgmental environment, emphasizing that feedback serves as a catalyst for development rather than punishment.

Strategic Communication Channels

In today's interconnected world, leaders have an array of communication channels at their disposal. However, wise leaders understand that not all channels are equally effective in different situations.

Face-to-face communication remains one of the most powerful modes of communication. It allows leaders to establish personal connections and convey emotions effectively. While face-to-face communication may not always be possible, especially in large organizations or geographically dispersed teams, leaders should make an effort to engage in regular in-person meetings whenever possible.

In addition to face-to-face communication, leaders must leverage technology to enhance their communication reach. Email, instant messaging, and video conferencing platforms serve as valuable tools for bridging communication gaps, particularly for remote teams. Leaders should adapt their communication style to the chosen channel, ensuring their messages are concise, relevant, and tailored to the audience.

Cultural Sensitivity

In today's globalized workplace, leaders often lead diverse teams with members from different cultural backgrounds. Cultural sensitivity is crucial for effective leadership communication in such environments. Leaders must strive to understand and respect cultural differences to avoid misunderstandings, conflicts, or biases.

To enhance cultural sensitivity, leaders should educate themselves on the diverse cultural values, customs, and communication styles within their teams. They should adapt their communication strategies to accommodate these differences and foster an inclusive and collaborative environment. Acknowledging and valuing diverse perspectives leads to improved communication outcomes and team productivity.

Transparency and Authenticity

A critical aspect of successful leadership communication is transparency and authenticity. Leaders who are transparent instill trust and loyalty within their teams by providing honest and open information about organizational decisions, challenges, and opportunities.

Authenticity is equally important in leadership communication. Leaders must project their true selves and not attempt to be someone they are not. Authentic leaders are genuine, open, and honest in their interactions, which makes it easier for their teams to relate to them and connect on a deeper level. Authentic leaders inspire loyalty and commitment, creating a positive and engaged work environment.

Non-Verbal Communication

While verbal language is essential, non-verbal communication often conveys more meaning than words alone. Leaders must be cognizant of their non-verbal cues and use them intentionally to strengthen their message.

Non-verbal communication includes facial expressions, body language, gestures, and tone of voice. Leaders must ensure their non-verbal cues align with their verbal message to avoid confusion or mixed signals. Maintaining eye contact, using appropriate hand gestures, and demonstrating open and confident body language can significantly enhance the impact of a leader's communication.

Leadership communication is a complex and multifaceted process that requires continuous learning and refinement. Successful leaders understand the power of clear and engaging communication, active listening, strategic communication channels, cultural sensitivity, transparency and authenticity, and non-verbal communication.

By implementing these communication strategies effectively, leaders can build strong relationships, inspire their teams, and achieve desired outcomes. However, it is important to remember that effective communication is a journey, not a destination. Leaders must commit to ongoing practice and improvement to ensure their communication remains relevant and impactful in an ever-evolving work environment.

In any team or group setting, conflict is bound to arise. The presence of diverse personalities, perspectives, and opinions can often lead to disagreements, tension, and challenges. However, conflict, when managed effectively, can be a catalyst for growth, creativity, and innovation within teams. This chapter aims to explore the various aspects of conflict management, including its definition, understanding conflict styles, and providing strategies to effectively manage conflict within teams.

Defining Conflict

Conflict can be broadly defined as a disagreement or struggle between two or more individuals arising from differences in objectives, opinions, or methods. It is important to note that not all conflict is negative; constructive conflict can foster collaboration, shared learning, and creativity within teams. However, destructive conflict can have detrimental effects on team dynamics, productivity, and morale.

Understanding Conflict Styles

To effectively manage conflict within teams, it is crucial to understand different conflict styles and how they can influence interpersonal relationships. There are various conflict management models, and one of the most well-known is the Thomas-Kilmann Conflict Mode Instrument (TKI).

The TKI model identifies five primary conflict styles:

1. Competing: This style is characterized by high assertiveness and low cooperation. Individuals using this style tend to prioritize their own goals and interests over others. While useful in certain situations, overreliance on this style can lead to hostility within the team.

2. Collaborating: Collaborating involves high assertiveness and high cooperation. This conflict style emphasizes the needs and interests of all team members and aims to find win-win solutions. Collaboration fosters open communication, creativity, and trust within teams.

3. Compromising: This style involves moderate assertiveness and cooperation. Individuals using this style seek to find middle-ground solutions where each party compromises to some extent. Compromising can be a useful approach when a quick resolution is needed or when both parties have equally important goals.

4. Avoiding: Avoiding is characterized by low assertiveness and cooperation. This conflict style involves individuals sidestepping disagreements, either by avoiding the issue altogether or deferring it to a later time. While avoiding can temporarily reduce tension,

unresolved conflicts may resurface or escalate later.

5. Accommodating: Accommodating involves low assertiveness and high cooperation. Individuals using this style prioritize the needs and interests of others over their own. Accommodation is beneficial when the issue at hand is of greater importance to another team member or when preserving harmony is crucial.

Each of these conflict styles has its strengths and weaknesses, and the most effective approach to conflict management depends on the situation, the individuals involved, and the team's overall goals.

Strategies for Managing Conflict

1. Encourage open communication: Create an environment where team members feel safe and encouraged to express their viewpoints without fear of retribution. Active listening, empathy, and open-mindedness are crucial to fostering this type of communication.

2. Identify the root cause: Explore the underlying causes of the conflict rather than focusing solely on the surface-level disagreement. Understanding the underlying needs, values, and interests of each team member can enable the identification of mutually agreeable solutions.

3. Foster a culture of respect and empathy: Encourage team

members to demonstrate respect and empathy towards one another. Promote the understanding that differing opinions and perspectives contribute to the overall success of the team.

4. Encourage diverse perspectives: Embrace diversity within the team and recognize that varying opinions and perspectives can lead to better collective decision-making. Encouraging team members to share their unique viewpoints can reduce conflict and foster innovative thinking.

5. Develop conflict resolution skills: Provide training and resources to team members to enhance their conflict resolution skills. This may include workshops, seminars, or coaching sessions that focus on effective communication, negotiation, and problem-solving.

6. Mediation and facilitation: In more complex or deeply-rooted conflicts, consider bringing in a mediator or facilitator to help navigate the discussion and find common ground. A neutral third-party can provide an unbiased perspective and guide the team towards a resolution.

7. Establish team norms and guidelines: Create clear expectations and guidelines for team behavior, conflict resolution processes, and decision-making. These norms and guidelines act as a reference point during conflicts, ensuring everyone understands the agreed-upon procedures.

8. Encourage feedback and reflection: The team should regularly evaluate how conflicts are managed and resolved. Encourage team members to provide feedback on their experiences and reflect on ways to improve conflict management moving forward.

Conflict within teams is a natural and inevitable occurrence. By understanding the different conflict styles and implementing effective strategies, conflict can be transformed into an opportunity for growth, learning, and collaboration within teams. Open communication, respect for diversity, and the development of conflict resolution skills are essential elements in building strong and successful teams that can effectively navigate and manage conflicts.

Chapter 3: Developing Personal Leadership Traits

In today's fast-paced and constantly evolving world, leadership has become an essential quality, not only in business but also in our personal lives. Leadership is about inspiring and guiding others towards a common goal, and it requires a unique set of traits and skills. In this chapter, we will delve into the topic of developing personal leadership traits, exploring the foundational qualities that lay the groundwork for effective leadership. Let us embark on this journey of self-discovery and growth as we unlock the secrets to becoming a remarkable leader.

Self-Awareness: The Key to Unleashing Leadership Potential

It all starts with self-awareness. The ability to understand and recognize our own strengths, weaknesses, emotions, and values is the cornerstone of personal leadership development. Without self-awareness, leaders may find it challenging to make informed decisions and effectively connect with their teams.

Self-awareness involves taking an honest inventory of our personality traits, habits, and beliefs. It requires self-reflection, being open to feedback, and continuously seeking self-improvement. By understanding ourselves better, we can identify areas for growth and leverage our strengths to lead others more effectively.

Building Emotional Intelligence for Impactful Leadership

Alongside self-awareness, emotional intelligence plays a vital role in shaping our leadership abilities. Emotional intelligence (EI) refers to the capacity to recognize, understand, and manage our own emotions, as well as empathize with others. It involves self-control, self-motivation, social skills, and empathy.

Leaders with high emotional intelligence can navigate challenging situations with grace, remain calm under pressure, and inspire others to perform at their best. They cultivate positive relationships and build trust within their teams. Developing emotional intelligence involves actively listening to others, expressing empathy, and being mindful of our own emotions. It is a lifelong journey that requires consistent practice and self-reflection.

The Power of Vision: Creating a Compelling Future

Leadership without a clear vision is like a ship without a rudder. A compelling vision serves as a guiding star, providing direction and purpose to both individuals and teams. It enables leaders to rally their followers and align efforts towards a common goal.

Developing a vision requires a deep understanding of oneself, the organization, and the external environment. It involves envisioning possibilities, thinking creatively, and setting ambitious yet attainable goals. A well-communicated vision inspires and energizes others, fostering commitment and dedication to the shared objectives.

Cultivating Effective Communication Skills

Communication is the lifeblood of effective leadership. Leaders must be adept at conveying ideas, motivating others, and fostering collaboration within their teams. They must cultivate an environment where open and transparent communication thrives.

Exceptional communicators master both verbal and non-verbal communication methods. They actively listen to understand, ask thoughtful questions, and provide constructive feedback. They adapt their communication style to different situations and individuals to ensure their message resonates with their audience.

Developing communication skills requires practice, self-awareness, and empathy. Leaders must create a safe space where everyone feels comfortable expressing themselves, resulting in open dialogue and increased engagement.

Building a Growth Mindset for Continuous Improvement

A growth mindset is the belief that abilities and intelligence can be developed through dedication, effort, and continuous learning. Leaders with a growth mindset embrace challenges, persist in the face of setbacks, and view failures as opportunities for improvement.

To cultivate a growth mindset, leaders must be open to new ideas and perspectives. They should encourage curiosity and foster a culture of continuous learning within their teams. By seeking feedback, focusing on personal and professional development, and promoting a positive learning environment, leaders can propel themselves and their teams to new heights of success.

The Importance of Authenticity and Integrity

Leadership is not merely about the application of skills; it is a reflection of one's character. Authenticity and integrity are foundational traits that build trust and credibility with others. Authentic leaders are true to themselves and their values. They are transparent, genuine, and not afraid to show vulnerability. By embracing their true selves, they inspire others to do the same, fostering an environment where everyone can bring their whole selves to work.

Integrity is the alignment of words and actions with ethical principles. Leaders with integrity prioritize doing what is right, even when it is difficult or unpopular. They lead by example and set high moral standards for others to follow.

Recognizing and Cultivating Self-awareness

In today's fast-paced and ever-evolving world, finding time to pause and reflect on oneself has become increasingly challenging. Amidst constant distractions and the demands of modern life, many individuals find themselves disconnected from their true selves, often leading to stress, anxiety, and a general sense of dissatisfaction. Recognizing and cultivating self-awareness is the key to breaking free from this cycle. In this chapter, we will explore the concept of self-awareness, its significance, and practical strategies to develop and nurture it.

Understanding Self-Awareness:

Self-awareness can be defined as the ability to objectively observe and understand oneself, including one's emotions, thoughts, behaviors, and overall identity. It is a critical component of emotional intelligence and serves as a foundation for personal growth and transformation. By becoming self-aware, we gain a deeper understanding of our strengths, weaknesses, values, beliefs, and motivations, enabling us to make conscious choices aligned with our authentic selves.

The Benefits of Self-Awareness:

1. Enhanced Emotional Intelligence: Self-awareness allows us to recognize and understand our emotions, ultimately leading to better self-regulation and improved interpersonal relationships. When we are aware of our emotional triggers, we can respond rather than react impulsively, fostering empathy and effective communication with others.

2. Improved Decision-Making: When we understand ourselves deeply, we are better equipped to make choices aligned with our values, aspirations, and long-term goals. Self-awareness helps us identify our biases and challenges our limiting beliefs, enabling us to make informed decisions that are in line with our authentic selves.

3. Increased Resilience: Self-awareness allows us to identify our strengths and weaknesses, enabling us to focus on personal growth and build resilience. By acknowledging our limitations and areas for improvement, we can harness our strengths and work towards becoming the best version of ourselves, even in the face of adversity.

Recognizing the Barriers to Self-Awareness:

Despite its numerous benefits, self-awareness is a lifelong journey that requires intentional effort. There are several common barriers that hinder our ability to recognize and cultivate it:

1. Denial: Sometimes, we might be uncomfortable facing our own flaws and vulnerabilities. Denial prevents us from introspecting and acknowledging areas of improvement, slowing down our personal growth.

2. Distractions: Modern life is full of distractions, ranging from social media to work pressures. These distractions can keep us in a constant state of busyness, making it difficult to find the time and space to reflect on ourselves.

3. Fear of Judgment: We often fear being judged by others or even ourselves. This fear can prevent us from exploring our inner selves and embracing all aspects of our personality, hindering the journey towards self-awareness.

Strategies to Cultivate Self-Awareness:

1. Mindfulness Practices: Mindfulness is the practice of being fully present in the moment, without judgment. Engaging in daily mindfulness practices such as meditation, deep breathing, or journaling can help in developing self-awareness. By observing our thoughts, emotions, and physical sensations without attachment, we can cultivate a deeper connection with ourselves.

2. Seeking Feedback: Actively seeking feedback from trusted individuals can provide valuable insights into our blind spots.

Genuine feedback helps us understand how our actions and behaviors impact others, fostering personal growth and awareness.

3. Journaling: Maintaining a reflective journal allows us to record our thoughts, emotions, and experiences. This practice helps us identify patterns, triggers, and recurring themes, ultimately leading to a deeper understanding of ourselves.

4. Self-Reflection: Carving out regular time for self-reflection is crucial. This can be achieved through practices such as solitude, going for walks in nature, or engaging in mindfulness exercises. By intentionally creating space for introspection, we allow ourselves to explore our inner thoughts, beliefs, and values.

5. Emotional Awareness: Cultivating emotional intelligence requires recognizing, labeling, and understanding our emotions. Paying close attention to our emotional experiences, practicing emotional regulation techniques, and exploring the root causes of our emotions can deepen our self-awareness.

6. Values Clarification: Examining and clarifying our core values enables us to understand what truly matters to us. By identifying our values, we can align our choices, actions, and behaviors with our authentic selves, enhancing our self-awareness and overall well-being.

Recognizing and cultivating self-awareness requires continuous effort, patience, and commitment.

By persistently engaging in practices such as mindfulness, seeking feedback, journaling, self-reflection, and values clarification, we can bridge the gap between who we think we are and who we truly are.

This journey towards self-awareness not only empowers us to make conscious choices and live authentic lives, but it also lays the foundation for personal growth, improved relationships, and overall well-being. Embracing self-awareness can truly transform our lives, allowing us to become more in tune with ourselves and the world around us.

Emotional Intelligence in Leadership

Leadership is an art that requires a delicate balance between rational decision-making and understanding human emotions. In the modern world, where organizations are becoming more complex and diverse, emotional intelligence has emerged as a crucial trait for effective leadership. Emotional intelligence refers to the ability to recognize and manage emotions, both in oneself and in others, to enhance relationships, make sound decisions, and achieve organizational goals. This chapter explores the significance of emotional intelligence in leadership, its components, and how it can be developed and applied in practice.

Understanding Emotional Intelligence

Emotional intelligence encompasses a range of critical skills that allow leaders to navigate the complex dynamics of human emotions. Although traditional leadership theories focused primarily on cognitive abilities and technical skills, it is now widely recognized that emotional intelligence is equally essential for effective leadership. Research shows that leaders with high emotional intelligence are more likely to inspire trust, build strong relationships, and foster a positive work culture.

Components of Emotional Intelligence

To fully grasp the concept of emotional intelligence in leadership, it is essential to understand its components. The most widely accepted framework, proposed by Daniel Goleman, suggests that emotional intelligence comprises five key dimensions:

1. Self-Awareness: Leaders with high self-awareness are conscious of their own emotions, strengths, weaknesses, and their impact on others. They have a deep understanding of their values, beliefs, and motivations, which enables them to make authentic and informed decisions.

2. Self-Regulation: Effective leaders possess the ability to control and manage their emotions even in challenging situations. They exhibit resilience, remain calm under pressure, and resist impulsive reactions. By regulating their emotions, leaders can create a conducive environment for open communication and problem-solving.

3. Motivation: Leaders with high emotional intelligence are driven by a genuine passion for their work and possess a strong sense of purpose. They set challenging goals, demonstrate enthusiasm, and inspire their team members to achieve excellence. Motivated leaders create a positive and energizing workplace atmosphere, leading to increased productivity.

4. Empathy: Empathy is the ability to understand and share the emotions of others. Leaders who possess empathy connect with their team members on a deeper level, demonstrating genuine care and consideration. They listen attentively, value diverse perspectives, and foster an environment of inclusivity, leading to improved collaboration and employee satisfaction.

5. Social Skills: Strong social skills allow leaders to effectively communicate, inspire, and influence others. Leaders with high social competence excel in building relationships, resolving conflicts, and creating a culture of trust and cooperation. They exhibit effective teamwork and provide constructive feedback, enabling their team members to grow and succeed.

Developing Emotional Intelligence in Leadership

While some individuals may possess a natural inclination towards emotional intelligence, it is a skill that can be developed and enhanced over time. Here are some strategies for developing emotional intelligence in leadership:

1. Self-Reflection: Engage in regular self-reflection to identify patterns, triggers, and emotional responses. Journaling or seeking feedback from trusted colleagues can provide valuable insights into one's emotional strengths and areas for improvement.

2. Emotional Awareness: Pay attention to emotions, both in oneself and in others. Practice recognizing different emotions and their impact on behavior and decision-making. This awareness will heighten emotional intelligence and support better understanding of others' perspectives.

3. Active Listening: Cultivate active listening skills to truly understand others' emotions, concerns, and needs. This shows empathy and allows leaders to respond appropriately, building rapport and connection with team members.

4. Managing Stress: Develop strategies to manage stress effectively. Regular exercise, mindfulness techniques, and maintaining a healthy work-life balance can help leaders regulate their own emotions and positively influence their team's emotional states.

5. Feedback and Coaching: Seek feedback and coaching from trusted mentors or professional coaches to gain insights into blind spots and areas for development. Objective feedback can provide invaluable guidance for self-improvement.

The Impact of Emotional Intelligence in Leadership

Leaders who possess high emotional intelligence are known to create productive and thriving work environments. Here are some key impacts of emotional intelligence in leadership:

1. Enhanced Communication: Leaders with strong emotional intelligence communicate effectively and adapt their communication style to best suit their team members' needs. This results in improved collaboration, fewer misunderstandings, and increased

engagement.

2. Increased Employee Engagement: Leaders who demonstrate empathy, motivation, and understanding significantly impact employee engagement. When employees feel seen, heard, and valued, they are more likely to be committed to their work, leading to higher levels of productivity and retention.

3. Conflict Resolution: Leaders with high emotional intelligence excel in managing and resolving conflicts. They approach conflicts with empathy, understanding, and consideration, finding win-win solutions that satisfy all parties. This results in a harmonious work environment, fostering stronger teamwork and collaboration.

4. Effective Decision-Making: Emotional intelligence enables leaders to make rational decisions while considering the emotions and perspectives of others. This leads to more comprehensive problem-solving, as leaders can weigh the impact their decisions will have on the team's morale and motivation.

Emotional intelligence plays a pivotal role in effective leadership. While technical expertise and cognitive abilities are essential, it is emotional intelligence that separates exceptional leaders from the rest. By focusing on developing self-awareness, self-regulation, empathy, motivation, and social skills, leaders can unlock their full emotional potential and inspire greatness in themselves and their teams. Embracing emotional intelligence in leadership is no longer a choice; it is a necessity for success in today's dynamic and ever-evolving business world.

Building Resilience and Adaptability

Resilience is the ability to bounce back from adversity, overcome challenges, and adapt to change. In a world constantly evolving, resilience has become a crucial skill for individuals and organizations alike. It is the key to not only surviving but thriving in the face of uncertainty and setbacks. In this chapter, we will delve into the concept of resilience, exploring its importance, characteristics, and strategies to build resilience.

1.1 The Importance of Resilience

Resilience is essential for our well-being and success in navigating life's ups and downs. It allows us to recover from failure, learn from experiences, and remain optimistic in the face of adversity. Resilient individuals demonstrate higher levels of mental and emotional well-being, show improved problem-solving skills, and are better equipped to handle stress.

In today's fast-paced and unpredictable world, where change is constant, building resilience is no longer an option but a necessity. From personal crises like the loss of a loved one to global challenges such as the COVID-19 pandemic, resilient individuals and organizations are better prepared to adapt and thrive amidst adversity.

1.2 Characteristics of Resilient Individuals

Resilient individuals possess certain characteristics that enable them to navigate challenging situations with strength and determination. These characteristics include:

1.2.1 Self-Awareness: Resilient individuals have a deep understanding of their emotions, strengths, and weaknesses. They can recognize their triggers and develop effective coping mechanisms.

1.2.2 Optimism: Resilient individuals maintain an optimistic outlook, believing in their ability to overcome obstacles. They see setbacks as temporary and maintain hope for the future.

1.2.3 Adaptability: Resilient individuals are flexible and open to change. They can adjust their strategies and perspectives to align with new circumstances.

1.2.4 Problem-solving skills: Resilient individuals possess strong problem-solving skills. They approach challenges with a growth mindset, seeking solutions and learning from their experiences.

1.2.5 Social support: Resilient individuals understand the importance of social connections. They seek and offer support to others, fostering a community of resilience.

1.3 Strategies for Building Resilience

While some individuals may naturally possess resilience, it is a skill that can be developed and strengthened over time. Here are some strategies to build resilience:

1.3.1 Cultivate a positive mindset: Adopting a positive mindset creates a mental framework that helps individuals see opportunities rather than obstacles. Engaging in positive self-talk, practicing gratitude, and reframing negative situations can all contribute to building a resilient mindset.

1.3.2 Develop emotional intelligence: Emotional intelligence allows individuals to understand and manage their emotions effectively. By developing self-awareness and empathy for others, individuals can build resilience and navigate challenges with grace.

1.3.3 Foster healthy coping mechanisms: Engaging in healthy coping mechanisms such as exercise, mindfulness, and creative outlets can help regulate emotions and reduce stress. These activities provide individuals with a constructive way to manage adversity.

1.3.4 Seek social support: Building a strong support network is crucial for resilience. Seeking support from friends, family, or professionals can provide the guidance and encouragement needed during difficult times.

1.3.5 Learn from setbacks: Resilient individuals view setbacks as opportunities for growth. They view failure as a stepping stone on the path to success and use it as a chance to learn, adapt, and improve.

Chapter 2: The Power of Adaptability

Adaptability is closely intertwined with resilience. It is the ability to adjust and respond effectively to new circumstances, challenges, and opportunities. In this chapter, we will explore the art of adaptability, its significance, and strategies to enhance adaptability in our lives.

2.1 Understanding Adaptability

Adaptability is the hallmark of successful individuals and organizations. With rapidly changing technologies, evolving markets, and shifting priorities, the ability to adapt has become a competitive advantage. Adaptability allows individuals and organizations to stay relevant, remain ahead of the curve, and seize new opportunities.

2.2 The Benefits of Adaptability

Being adaptable offers several benefits, both in personal and professional settings:

2.2.1 Embracing Change: Adaptable individuals embrace change rather than fearing it. They are open to new ideas and experiences, making them more versatile and capable of navigating unfamiliar territories.

2.2.2 Improved Problem-solving: Adaptable individuals possess a diverse set of skills and perspectives. They are better equipped to analyze problems from multiple angles, find innovative solutions, and think outside the box.

2.2.3 Enhanced Resilience: Adaptability and resilience go hand in hand. Individuals who can adapt to change are more likely to bounce back from setbacks and triumph over adversity.

2.2.4 Increased Creativity: Adaptable individuals are natural creative thinkers. They can approach challenges with fresh eyes, exploring unconventional solutions and unlocking their creative potential.

2.3 Strategies for Enhancing Adaptability

Adaptability is a learnable trait that can be cultivated over time. Here are some strategies to enhance adaptability in your life:

2.3.1 Embrace continuous learning: Adaptability requires a mindset of constant growth and development. Embrace a love for learning, whether through formal education, reading, or seeking new experiences. Stay curious and open-minded.

2.3.2 Foster a growth mindset: Adopting a growth mindset allows individuals to see challenges as opportunities for growth and learning. Embrace the belief that abilities and intelligence can be developed through effort and practice.

2.3.3 Emphasize flexibility: Be open to change and willing to let go of routines or preconceived notions. Emphasize flexibility in your thoughts, actions, and decision-making processes.

2.3.4 Develop multi-disciplinary skills: Cultivate a diverse skill set that allows you to adapt to different roles and industries. Acquiring a broad range of skills increases your versatility and potential for success.

2.3.5 Embrace feedback: Seek feedback from others and be willing to incorporate it into your personal and professional development. Feedback provides valuable insights and helps identify areas for improvement.

Resilience and adaptability are not limited to individuals but also play a vital role in organizational success. In this chapter, we will explore how organizations can cultivate resilience and adaptability within their teams and structures.

3.1 Creating a Resilient Culture

Building a resilient culture starts with leadership and permeates across all levels of an organization. Here are some strategies to foster resilience within organizations:

3.1.1 Lead by example: Leaders set the tone for resilience. By demonstrating resilience in their own actions and decision-making, leaders inspire employees to do the same.

3.1.2 Promote open communication: Establish a culture of open and transparent communication, where employees feel comfortable sharing challenges, seeking support, and providing feedback. This creates a sense of psychological safety and encourages resilience.

3.1.3 Encourage continuous learning: Support and invest in employees' professional development. Provide opportunities for growth, training, and upskilling, encouraging a growth mindset and adaptability.

3.1.4 Celebrate successes and failures: Acknowledge individual and team accomplishments to create a positive work environment. Similarly, encourage learning from failures. Promote lessons learned and the development of effective strategies moving forward.

3.2 Fostering Adaptability

Organizational adaptability is essential for surviving and thriving in an ever-changing business landscape. Here are some strategies to enhance adaptability within organizations:

3.2.1 Encourage innovation and creativity: Foster an environment that encourages employees to think creatively and come up with innovative solutions. Provide outlets for experimentation and risk-taking.

3.2.2 Promote collaboration and cross-functional teams: Foster collaboration across departments and create opportunities for employees from different backgrounds to work together. This encourages the sharing of diverse perspectives and enhances adaptability.

3.2.3 Implement agile processes: Adopt agile methodologies and frameworks to increase responsiveness to change. Agile methodologies promote flexibility, continuous improvement, and quick decision-making.
3.2.4 Embrace technology and automation: Embracing technological advances can improve operational efficiency and allow organizations to adapt to changing market demands. Invest in technology that streamlines processes and enhances adaptability.

Leveraging Personal Values for Ethical Leadership

Ethical leadership is a concept that holds immense significance in today's globalized world, where organizations are expected to act with integrity and make decisions that benefit all stakeholders. While leadership styles may vary, one aspect that remains constant is the importance of personal values in guiding ethical decision-making. In this chapter, we will explore the role of personal values in ethical leadership and how leaders can leverage these values to create a positive impact on their teams, organizations, and society as a whole.

Defining Ethical Leadership:

Before delving deeper into the connection between personal values and ethical leadership, let's begin by understanding what ethical leadership truly means. Ethical leadership encompasses a set of moral principles and values that guide leaders in making decisions that are fair, just, and for the greater good. It involves acting in accordance with one's conscience, while considering ethical and moral implications in the decision-making process.

The Power of Personal Values:

Personal values are the core beliefs and principles that shape an individual's behavior, actions, and decisions. They serve as guiding forces in both personal and professional aspects of life. For leaders, understanding and aligning their personal values with their leadership style can significantly impact their ability to make ethically sound decisions.

Identifying Personal Values:

To leverage personal values for ethical leadership, leaders must first identify and define their personal values. This involves a deep introspection of their core beliefs, what drives them, and what they stand for. In doing so, leaders can gain clarity on their values and develop a stronger sense of self-awareness. Important questions to ask oneself during this introspection include:

1. What principles do I hold dear?
2. What do I prioritize in both my personal and professional life?
3. What values do I want to embody as a leader?
4. How can I ensure consistency between my values and actions?

Aligning Personal and Organizational Values:

Once leaders have a clear understanding of their personal values, the next step is to align them with the values of the organization they lead. Organizations often have their own set of core values and a defined organizational culture that reflects what they stand for. Leaders must analyze the alignment between their personal values and the shared values of the organization and identify areas of congruence.

If personal and organizational values are well-aligned, leaders can leverage this alignment to influence their followers positively. Employees are more likely to trust and respect a leader who leads by example, demonstrating consistency between their personal values and the values promoted by the organization.

Living the Values:

Leveraging personal values for ethical leadership requires leaders to live and breathe their values in their day-to-day interactions and decision-making. It is essential for leaders to act as role models, consistently demonstrating behavior that aligns with their personal values. Employees are more likely to follow leaders who exhibit integrity, authenticity, and ethical behavior, fostering a healthy work environment where everyone feels valued and motivated.

Integrating Values into Decision-Making:

Ethical leadership involves incorporating personal values into the decision-making process. Values play a crucial role in guiding leaders when faced with complex dilemmas or challenging decisions. Leaders can evaluate potential courses of action against their personal values, considering the long-term impact on various stakeholders. This ensures that decisions are made not only based on short-term gains but also take into account the ethical dimension.

However, it is crucial to note that personal values should not be used as a justification for biased decision-making. Leaders must remain open to different perspectives and consider the broader ethical implications of their decisions. Balancing personal values with fairness, diversity, and inclusivity is essential for ethical leadership.

Fostering Ethical Organizational Culture:

Leaders who leverage their personal values for ethical leadership have the potential to influence and shape the organizational culture positively. By consistently demonstrating ethical behavior and decision-making, leaders set the tone for their teams and organizations, emphasizing the importance of integrity and accountability. This encourages employees to align their actions with ethical principles, fostering a culture of trust and respect.

Communicating Values:

Leaders' ability to effectively communicate their personal values is fundamental in leveraging them for ethical leadership. By openly sharing their values and the rationale behind their decisions, leaders create a transparent and inclusive environment where everyone is aware of the ethical standards expected within the organization. Effective communication helps employees understand the alignment between their personal values and the organization's values, enabling them to make ethical choices in their own work.

Leveraging personal values for ethical leadership is a continuous journey that requires self-reflection, self-awareness, and consistent commitment. When leaders authentically align their personal values with organizational values and demonstrate ethical behavior, they can cultivate a culture of integrity, trust, and accountability within their organizations. This ethical leadership, driven by personal values, has the potential to make a significant and positive impact on individuals, teams, organizations, and society as a whole. By embracing personal values, leaders can shape a better future, fostering a world where ethical principles and values drive decision-making and actions at all levels.

Chapter 4: Crafting a Visionary Path

Throughout the ages, visionary thinkers and leaders have shaped the course of history by envisioning a future that others could not yet see. They possess a unique ability to imagine possibilities beyond the constraints of the present and inspire others to follow their lead. Crafting a visionary path requires a combination of foresight, creativity, and relentless pursuit of a grand vision that goes beyond personal gain. This chapter explores the characteristics and strategies employed by visionary individuals who have left an indelible mark on society.

1. The Power of Imagination

At the heart of crafting a visionary path lies the power of imagination. Visionaries possess a remarkable ability to visualize a future that exists only in their minds. They draw upon this vivid mental picture to create a compelling vision that transcends the boundaries of the present reality. Imagination serves as the catalyst for transformative change, fueling the motivation and determination necessary to bring their vision to life.

2. Defining a Compelling Vision

Crafting a visionary path begins with the development of a compelling vision. This vision serves as a guiding light, illuminating the path towards the desired future. A visionary leader must possess the clarity and conviction to articulate this vision in a way that resonates with others. By painting a vivid picture of what lies ahead, they inspire and mobilize individuals to embark on a collective journey towards a shared destination.

3. Thinking Beyond the Present

Visionaries possess an innate ability to transcend the limitations of the present. They refuse to be confined by current circumstances and conventional thinking. Instead, they continually push the boundaries of what is possible, challenging societal norms and envisioning a future that stretches beyond perceived limitations. By embracing a forward-thinking mindset, visionaries pave the way for innovation and progress.

4. Pathfinding and Goal Setting

Crafting a visionary path requires rigorous planning and goal setting. Visionaries embark on a journey of pathfinding, identifying the necessary steps and milestones required to bring their vision to fruition. They break down the grand vision into smaller, achievable goals, providing clear direction and purpose for themselves and those who join them on this transformative journey. Strategic goal setting ensures that progress is measurable, enabling visionaries to garner support and build momentum.

5. Harnessing the Power of Collaboration

Visionaries understand that the path to achieving their grand vision cannot be traveled alone. Collaboration becomes a cornerstone of their approach, as they rally individuals around a shared purpose and inspire them to contribute their unique talents towards the greater goal. By harnessing the collective intelligence and expertise of others, visionaries amplify their impact and foster a sense of ownership and belonging among their collaborators.

6. Resilience and Perseverance

Crafting a visionary path is often fraught with challenges and setbacks. Visionaries possess an unwavering determination and resilience in the face of adversity. They view obstacles as opportunities for growth and adaptation, remaining steadfast in their commitment to their vision. Their ability to maintain focus and persevere in the face of adversity creates an unwavering sense of purpose that fuels progress.

7. Inspiring and Mobilizing Others

A visionary leader's success lies in their ability to inspire and mobilize others towards a common purpose. They possess exceptional communication skills that allow them to translate their grand vision into a compelling narrative. By captivating the hearts and minds of individuals, visionaries create a sense of urgency and inspire action. They build a united front of passionate followers who share their unwavering commitment to realizing the envisioned future.

8. Adaptability and Embracing Change

Visionary individuals recognize the dynamic nature of the world around them. They remain flexible and adaptable, willing to adjust their course as circumstances evolve. They embrace change as an opportunity rather than a hindrance, leveraging it to their advantage and enhancing their ability to navigate towards their vision. This adaptability ensures that visionaries stay ahead of the curve and maintain their relevance in an ever-changing landscape.

9. Fostering a Legacy

Crafting a visionary path is not solely focused on personal achievements. Visionaries are motivated by a desire to leave a lasting legacy that inspires future generations. They invest in the development of those who will carry the torch forward, ensuring that their vision continues to shape a better future long after they are gone. This commitment to fostering a legacy sets visionary leaders apart, as their influence extends far beyond their own lifetime.

10. Balancing Vision and Execution

While visionaries possess an extraordinary ability to envision a better future, successful execution is equally crucial. They strike a delicate balance between dreaming big and executing with precision. By combining their visionary mindset with strategic thinking, they ensure that their grand vision is realized step by step. A visionary leader's ability to bridge the gap between vision and execution determines their long-term impact.

In conclusion, crafting a visionary path requires a unique blend of imagination, determination, collaboration, adaptability, and foresight. Visionaries possess an unwavering commitment to their grand vision and the ability to inspire and mobilize others towards its realization. By transcending the limitations of the present, they shape the course of history and leave behind a legacy that continues to transform the world.

Articulating a Compelling Vision

In the world of leadership and organizational management, one of the key skills that separates great leaders from the rest is their ability to articulate a compelling vision. A vision serves as a roadmap for an organization, providing a sense of direction, purpose, and motivation for employees and stakeholders. When a leader is able to convey this vision in a powerful and inspiring manner, it becomes a catalyst for change, inspiring individuals and teams to work towards a shared goal. In this chapter, we will explore the art of articulating a compelling vision and the impact it can have on organizational success.

Understanding the Power of Vision:

At its core, a vision represents a desirable future state that an organization aspires to achieve. It provides a clear picture of what success looks like and sets the tone for strategic planning, decision-making, and resource allocation. Without a compelling vision, organizations can become lost, as employees lack a sense of purpose and direction. A well-articulated vision acts as a lighthouse, guiding every action and decision towards the desired destination.

The Characteristics of a Compelling Vision:

A compelling vision possesses several key characteristics that make it powerful and inspiring. Firstly, it should be aspirational, stretching the organization beyond its current capabilities. It must challenge the status quo and ignite a sense of ambition and drive. Secondly, a vision should be unifying, bringing people together under a common goal. It must resonate with employees at all levels, providing a sense of belonging and shared purpose. Lastly, a compelling vision should be specific and measurable, allowing progress to be tracked and celebrated. It should not be generic or vague, but rather provide a clear target for success.

Crafting a Compelling Vision Statement:

A vision statement is the overarching expression of an organization's future aspirations. Crafting one requires a thoughtful and deliberate approach to ensure it captures the essence of the desired future state. To create a compelling vision statement, leaders should consider the following steps:

1. Reflect on the organization's identity and values:

A vision statement should align with the organization's core values and identity. Leaders must reflect on what the organization stands for and how it aims to make a positive impact on the world. This reflection will provide the foundation for the vision statement.

2. Engage stakeholders in the process:

Vision creation is not a solitary task; it requires input from various stakeholders. Leaders should engage employees, customers, and other key stakeholders to gain diverse perspectives and generate buy-in. Involving others in the process fosters a sense of ownership and commitment towards the vision.

3. Be future-oriented and ambitious:

A compelling vision stretches the organization beyond its comfort zone. Leaders should envision a future that challenges the organization to accomplish greatness. By setting ambitious goals, leaders inspire their teams to reach for new heights.

4. Ensure clarity and simplicity:

While the vision must be aspirational, it should also be clear and concise. Ambiguity and complexity can hinder understanding and alignment. Leaders must strive to communicate the vision in simple terms that resonate with everyone in the organization.

5. Test and refine the vision statement:

A vision statement is not set in stone. Leaders should test it against the organization's realities and context. This iterative process allows for fine-tuning the vision until it feels compelling and authentic.

Communicating the Vision:

Crafting a compelling vision statement is only the first step. Leaders must also effectively communicate the vision to ensure widespread understanding, engagement, and commitment. Here are some key strategies for communicating a vision:

1. Storytelling:

Humans are hardwired to connect with stories. Leaders should use storytelling techniques to convey the vision in a way that captivates and resonates with their audience. Stories help paint a vivid picture of the desired future and evoke emotional responses that drive action.

2. Paint a vivid picture:

Words alone are often insufficient to convey a vision. Leaders should use visuals, metaphors, and examples to paint a vivid picture of what success looks like. This helps people visualize the destination and fosters a shared understanding.

3. Repeated and consistent messaging:

Consistency is paramount when communicating the vision. Leaders should ensure that the vision is communicated through various channels repeatedly. Repetition helps reinforce the message and keeps the vision at the forefront of employees' minds.

4. Engage in dialogue:

Vision communication should be a two-way process. Leaders should actively engage in dialogue with employees, encouraging questions, feedback, and discussion. This interactive approach deepens understanding and fosters a sense of ownership.

5. Lead by example:

To inspire others, leaders must demonstrate their own commitment to the vision. Through their actions and decisions, leaders should embody the values and direction outlined in the vision statement. Leading by example builds trust and credibility, enhancing the vision's impact.

Aligning Actions and Systems:

An articulated vision statement alone is insufficient for driving organizational success. Leaders must align their actions, processes, and systems with the desired future state to enable the vision's fulfillment.

1. Goal-setting and performance measurement:

Organizational and individual goals should align with the vision. By setting clear and measurable objectives that support the vision, leaders ensure that everyone is working towards the same destination. Regular performance measurement helps track progress and identifies areas for improvement.

2. Decision-making and resource allocation:

Vision-driven decision-making involves evaluating options in light of the vision statement. Leaders must prioritize initiatives and allocate resources based on their alignment with the desired future state. This ensures that resources are invested in areas that contribute to the vision's realization.

3. Organizational structure and culture:

Leaders should consider adapting the organizational structure and culture to support the vision. Structures and cultures that hinder progress or create barriers need to be reevaluated and aligned with the vision's values and principles.

4. Communication and knowledge sharing:

Consistent communication channels and knowledge-sharing mechanisms should be established to keep employees informed about progress and align their efforts. Transparent and open communication helps foster a shared understanding of how individual contributions contribute to the bigger picture.

Articulating a compelling vision is undoubtedly a skill that distinguishes great leaders. As you have discovered in this chapter, a vision provides purpose, inspiration, and a sense of direction for organizations. Crafting a compelling vision requires thoughtful reflection, engagement of stakeholders, and clear communication. By aligning actions and systems with the vision, leaders set their organizations on a path towards success. As you move forward, remember that a compelling vision is not static; it must be revisited, refined, and communicated consistently to keep it alive and relevant in the minds and hearts of all those involved.

Setting SMART Goals for the Team

In every team, setting goals is crucial for success. It provides a clear direction, focus, and motivation for team members. However, not all goals are created equal. To ensure maximum efficiency and productivity, goals need to be SMART - specific, measurable, attainable, relevant, and time-bound. In this chapter, we will explore the concept of SMART goals and how they can be effectively implemented within a team to achieve desired outcomes.

Section 1: The Importance of Setting Goals

1.1 Understanding the Significance of Goals

Goals serve as a roadmap, guiding individuals and teams towards their desired objectives. Without clear goals, teams may struggle to stay focused, lack motivation, and experience difficulties in measuring progress. As the famous saying goes, "A goal without a plan is just a wish." It is through effective goal-setting techniques that teams can transform their aspirations into reality.

1.2 Establishing a Sense of Purpose

Setting goals provides individuals with a sense of purpose and direction. It helps team members align their efforts, energies, and talents towards a common objective. When everyone is working towards a shared vision, it fosters unity, collaboration, and enhances overall team morale.

Section 2: Understanding SMART Goals

2.1 Specific Goals

The first element of the SMART framework is specificity. Goals need to be clearly defined, leaving no room for ambiguity. A specific goal answers the 'what,' 'why,' 'who,' 'where,' and 'how' of the task at hand. For example, instead of setting a broad goal like "Increase sales," a specific goal would be "Increase monthly sales revenue by 15% within the next quarter."

2.2 Measurable Goals

Measurability is essential for tracking progress and evaluating success. Goals must be quantifiable, providing a tangible benchmark against which accomplishments can be gauged. Measurable goals enable teams to monitor their performance, make necessary adjustments, and celebrate milestones. For instance, a measurable goal could be "Increase customer satisfaction rating from 85% to 90% in the next six months."

2.3 Attainable Goals

While setting ambitious goals is valuable to drive growth, they must be attainable. Attainability ensures that the goals set are within reach, given the available resources, skill sets, and timeframe. Unrealistic goals can lead to frustration, demotivation, and ultimately, failure. Striking a balance between ambition and achievability ensures that teams are inspired to reach their full potential without setting themselves up for disappointment.

2.4 Relevant Goals

Relevance is the fourth aspect of SMART goals. Goals should align with the team's overall purpose and objectives. This ensures that efforts are directed towards meaningful outcomes that contribute to the team's success. Setting irrelevant goals can cause distraction, inefficiency, and waste of valuable resources. Therefore, it is essential to regularly evaluate the relevance of goals to maintain focus and maximize productivity.

2.5 Time-Bound Goals

Time-bound goals have a clear deadline or timeline attached to them. This element adds a sense of urgency and accountability to the goal-setting process. By setting specific time frames, teams can stay on track, prioritize tasks effectively, and avoid procrastination. Time-bound goals create a sense of structure and help teams maintain momentum, pushing them closer to their objectives.

Section 3: Strategies for Setting SMART Goals for Teams

3.1 Creating a Goal-Setting Framework

Implementing SMART goals within a team requires a systematic approach. Start by establishing a goal-setting framework that outlines the key components of the process. This framework can be shared with all team members to ensure a cohesive understanding of goal-setting expectations. Encourage team members to actively participate in the creation of this framework, fostering a sense of ownership and engagement.

3.2 Encouraging Collaboration

Goal setting should not be a one-size-fits-all process. Involve the entire team in goal-setting discussions to promote collaboration and diversity of ideas. This collaborative approach fosters a sense of ownership and commitment while encouraging team members to contribute their unique perspectives. Through open dialogue and brainstorming sessions, the team can collectively define SMART goals that align with their shared vision.

3.3 Aligning Individual and Team Goals

While team goals are critical, it is equally important to align them with individual aspirations. When team members see their personal goals reflected in the team's objectives, they are more likely to be motivated, engaged, and invested in the process. Encourage team members to identify their individual goals and find ways to align them with the team's broader goals. This synchronization creates a supportive environment where individuals can work towards their personal growth while contributing to the team's success.

3.4 Breaking Down Goals into Actionable Steps

SMART goals provide a structure for success, but translating them into actionable steps is equally crucial. Break down high-level goals into smaller, manageable tasks that can be achieved within a reasonable timeframe. This approach not only enhances productivity but also helps team members understand how their efforts contribute to the overall goal. Breaking down goals into smaller steps also makes it easier to measure progress and celebrate achievements along the way.

3.5 Regularly Reviewing and Adjusting Goals

Goal setting is not a one-time event but an ongoing process. Regularly review and assess the progress made towards achieving goals. Evaluate whether the established goals are still relevant, need adjustment or require new milestones. Encourage team members to provide feedback and suggestions, considering their valuable insights to modify goals as needed. This regular review and adjustment ensure that goals remain aligned with the team's evolving needs, enhancing overall effectiveness.

Setting SMART goals is a fundamental aspect of team success. By incorporating the principles of specificity, measurability, attainability, relevance, and time-boundness, teams can set clear objectives that ignite motivation, drive progress, and ensure efficient allocation of resources. Remember, SMART goals are not static; they require continual evaluation, adjustment, and collaboration. With a well-defined goal-setting framework and a collective sense of purpose, teams can transform their aspirations into accomplishments, achieving remarkable results along the way.

Strategic Planning and Decision-Making

In today's rapidly changing and unpredictable business landscape, organizations face immense pressure to not only survive but thrive. To navigate these challenges successfully, strategic planning and effective decision-making play pivotal roles. This chapter explores the critical concepts and processes involved in strategic planning and decision-making, shedding light on their importance, challenges, and methodologies.

1. Defining Strategic Planning:

Strategic planning is the process of charting an organization's course by setting goals, identifying objectives, and defining the necessary actions to achieve them. It involves aligning an organization's resources, capabilities, and decision-making processes to achieve its long-term vision.

1.1 Importance of Strategic Planning:

Strategic planning provides an organization with a roadmap to success amidst an ever-changing business environment. It helps align various departments and teams toward a common purpose, enabling the achievement of shared goals. Additionally, strategic planning facilitates effective resource allocation and gives organizations a competitive edge by identifying opportunities and mitigating risks.

1.2 Challenges in Strategic Planning:

While strategic planning is crucial, it is not without its challenges. Organizations must grapple with uncertainties, complexity, and the need for constant adaptation. Balancing long-term goals with short-term realities can pose a significant challenge, as can managing diverse viewpoints and conflicting priorities within an organization. Moreover, considering external factors such as market trends, regulatory changes, and technological advancements adds complexity to the strategic planning process.

2. Strategic Decision-Making:

Strategic decision-making is an integral part of the strategic planning process. It involves identifying and evaluating multiple alternatives to make informed choices that align with an organization's long-term goals.

2.1 Factors Influencing Strategic Decision-Making:

Several factors influence strategic decision-making. Primarily, decision-makers need to consider the organization's internal resources, capabilities, and external environment. Analyzing market trends, competition, customer needs, and stakeholder expectations are critical in making sound strategic decisions. Additionally, cognitive biases, personal preferences, and risk perception can influence decision-makers, warranting a structured approach to avoid potential pitfalls.

2.2 Methodologies for Strategic Decision-Making:

Various methodologies and frameworks can assist decision-makers in making well-informed strategic choices. One such approach is the SWOT (Strengths, Weaknesses, Opportunities, Threats) analysis, which helps organizations assess internal capabilities and external environmental factors. Another widely used framework is Porter's Five Forces, which helps identify competitive forces at play in a particular industry. Additionally, scenario planning, decision trees, and cost-benefit analysis serve as invaluable tools to evaluate alternatives, risks, and potential outcomes.

3. Integrating Strategic Planning and Decision-Making:

Successful organizations realize the interdependent nature of strategic planning and decision-making. Integrating the two processes ensures that decisions align with strategic objectives and contribute to the overall success of the organization.

3.1 Creating a Strategic Planning Framework:

Organizations can develop a strategic planning framework to streamline decision-making processes. By clearly defining the mission, vision, and values, an organization can establish a framework that guides strategic choices. Defining strategic objectives, setting performance metrics, and conducting regular reviews further contribute to an effective planning process.

3.2 Decision-Making Support Systems:

Decision-making support systems (DMSS) leverage modern technologies to aid in the strategic decision-making process. These systems provide real-time data, analytics, and insights, empowering decision-makers with accurate information. DMSS also facilitate collaboration and knowledge exchange, ensuring decisions are made based on robust analysis and diverse perspectives.

4. Implementing and Adapting the Strategic Plan:

A well-crafted strategic plan is only effective if it is properly implemented and continuously adapted to changing circumstances. Successful implementation requires effective communication, resource allocation, and performance tracking.

4.1 Communication and Alignment:

Clear and consistent communication is crucial throughout the implementation process. Ensuring all stakeholders understand the strategic goals, their roles, and responsibilities fosters collaboration and reinforces a shared vision. Continuous alignment with the broader organizational culture and values helps gain support from individuals at all levels, facilitating smoother implementation.

4.2 Monitoring and Adjusting:

Regular monitoring and tracking of progress against key performance indicators (KPIs) allow organizations to assess the effectiveness of their strategic plan. Adapting to changing market trends, technological advancements, and regulatory requirements requires flexibility and agility. Organizations must establish feedback mechanisms to capture insights from both internal and external sources, enabling timely adjustments to the strategic plan. Strategic planning and decision-making are vital components of organizational success. A well-crafted strategic plan, supported by effective decision-making, provides organizations with a roadmap to achieve their long-term objectives. Overcoming challenges, integrating these processes, and continuously adapting to a dynamic business environment enables organizations to stay ahead of the curve and seize opportunities. By embracing strategic planning and decision-making as ongoing practices, organizations can shape their own destinies and unlock their fullest potential.

Inspiring and Motivating Teams towards the Vision

In today's fast-paced and competitive business environment, organizations rely heavily on the collective efforts and synergy of their teams to achieve their vision. A team that is inspired and motivated towards the vision can accomplish extraordinary things, exceed expectations, and drive innovation. However, inspiring and motivating a team is not a one-time event; it is an ongoing process that requires dedication, effective communication, and strong leadership. In this chapter, we will delve into various strategies and techniques to inspire and motivate teams towards the vision, ultimately fostering growth and success within the organization.

Setting a Compelling Vision

At the core of inspiring and motivating teams lies a compelling vision that captures the hearts and minds of everyone involved. A vision serves as a guiding light, providing a clear direction and purpose to the team's efforts. When formulating a vision, it is important to make it meaningful, exciting, and feasible. A vision that is too vague or far-fetched can lead to disillusionment, while one that is too generic may fail to ignite passion.

To ensure that the team connects with the vision, leaders must involve them in the visioning process. Conducting brainstorming sessions or workshops where team members can contribute their ideas helps in creating a shared vision that everyone can get behind. Additionally, it is crucial to communicate the vision regularly and consistently, highlighting its importance and how it aligns with the team's individual and collective goals.

Fostering a Supportive Work Environment

In order to inspire and motivate teams towards the vision, it is essential to cultivate a supportive work environment that encourages growth, collaboration, and trust. When team members feel valued and supported, they are more likely to go the extra mile and contribute to the team's success. Here are some key elements to foster a supportive work environment:

1. Encouraging open communication: Creating an environment where team members are comfortable expressing their thoughts, ideas, and concerns without fear of judgment or retribution is vital. This promotes honest and transparent communication, fostering a sense of belonging and psychological safety within the team.

2. Recognizing and rewarding achievements: Acknowledging the hard work and accomplishments of team members is a powerful way to motivate and inspire. Regularly recognizing individuals and the collective team's efforts through praise, awards, or incentives fosters

a culture of appreciation and fuels intrinsic motivation.

3. Providing opportunities for growth and development: A team that is continuously learning and evolving is more likely to stay motivated and engaged. Offering training programs, professional development opportunities, and encouraging cross-functional collaboration are great ways to nurture personal and professional growth within the team.

Leading by Example

Leaders play a significant role in inspiring and motivating teams towards the vision. Team members often look up to their leaders for guidance and inspiration. Therefore, it is crucial for leaders to lead by example and exhibit the behaviors and values they expect from their team. Here are some key aspects of leading by example:

1. Demonstrating passion and commitment: Passion is contagious. When leaders are genuinely passionate about the vision, it resonates with the team and ignites their own enthusiasm. By demonstrating unwavering commitment to the vision, leaders inspire their teams to stay focused and dedicated.

2. Emphasizing trust and integrity: Trust is the foundation of any successful team. Leaders must prioritize building trust by being transparent, consistent, and honest in their actions and decisions. By

upholding integrity as a core value, leaders inspire their teams to do the same.

3. Encouraging innovation and risk-taking: A team constantly striving for improvement and innovation is more likely to achieve exceptional results. Leaders can motivate their teams by creating an environment that encourages experimentation, fosters creativity, and embraces calculated risks.

Effective Communication and Feedback

To inspire and motivate teams, effective communication is paramount. Clear, concise, and consistent communication helps ensure that the team understands the vision, goals, and expectations. Moreover, providing regular updates and progress reports creates a sense of purpose and keeps the team motivated. Here are some key communication strategies:

1. Share the big picture: Team members need context to understand how their individual tasks fit into the larger vision. By sharing the big picture and explaining the team's role within it, leaders can inspire a sense of purpose and significance.

2. Active listening: Listening empathetically to the team's ideas, concerns, and feedback is essential for creating a collaborative and supportive environment. By valuing their input, leaders show their

team that their voice matters and that their contributions are acknowledged.

3. Constructive feedback and recognition: Providing timely and specific feedback helps team members understand their areas of improvement and how they contribute to the team's vision. When feedback is balanced with regular recognition and appreciation for achievements, it motivates and inspires continuous growth.

Inspiring and motivating teams towards the vision is an ongoing process that requires a combination of effective leadership, supportive work environment, communication, and continuous learning. By setting a compelling vision, fostering teamwork, leading by example, and maintaining open lines of communication, leaders can unleash the full potential of their teams. A motivated and inspired team is not only more likely to achieve the organization's vision but also to exceed expectations, driving sustainable success and growth.

Chapter 5: Effective Communication Strategies

In today's fast-paced world, effective communication has become more important than ever. Whether it's in personal relationships, professional settings, or even on a global scale, good communication skills can make or break a situation. In this chapter, we will explore various strategies that can help you become a more effective communicator. We will delve into both verbal and non-verbal communication techniques, as well as the importance of active listening and empathy. Join us as we uncover the secrets to successful communication and unlock the doors to stronger connections with others.

The Power of Words:

Words have incredible power. They can heal, inspire, and motivate, but they can also hurt, discourage, and divide. Choosing our words carefully is vital to effective communication. The words we use not only convey our message but also shape how others perceive us.

One effective strategy is to use positive and affirming language. Instead of focusing on what we don't want, we can convey our desires and intentions in a more constructive manner. For example, rather than saying, "Don't be late," we can say, "Please arrive on time." This simple shift changes the focus from negativity to a positive expectation.

Another important aspect of verbal communication is tone. The same words can have completely different meanings depending on the tone in which they are delivered. A friendly and warm tone can create a sense of trust and openness, while a harsh or condescending tone can alienate and create tension. Being mindful of our tone and adapting it to the situation can significantly improve our communication effectiveness.

Beyond Words: Non-Verbal Communication:

Communication is not limited to words alone; non-verbal cues play a significant role in our interactions as well. Our facial expressions, gestures, body language, and even the way we dress all communicate messages to those around us.

One fundamental non-verbal communication strategy is maintaining good eye contact. Looking directly into someone's eyes while speaking shows our attentiveness and interest in the conversation. It also helps to establish a connection and build trust.

Similarly, our body language can either enhance or detract from our message. Standing or sitting up straight signifies confidence and engagement, while crossed arms or slouched posture might convey disinterest or defensiveness. Being aware of our body language and making conscious efforts to align it with our intended message can greatly improve the effectiveness of our communication.

Listening: The Key to Understanding:

Effective communication strategies not only involve speaking but also the art of listening. Unfortunately, many of us struggle with active listening. We often find ourselves thinking about how to respond or waiting for our turn to speak, instead of fully absorbing what the other person is saying.

Active listening is crucial for understanding and connecting with others. It involves giving our undivided attention, maintaining eye contact, and using verbal and non-verbal cues to show that we are engaged. Restating or paraphrasing what the speaker has said is also an effective way to ensure that we have understood the message correctly.

Empathy: Understanding the Other Perspective:

Empathy is an essential component of effective communication. Understanding others' perspectives, emotions, and experiences allows us to communicate in a way that resonates with them and builds stronger connections.

One way to practice empathy is by putting ourselves in the other person's shoes. Imagining their experiences, considering their emotions, and understanding their point of view enables us to respond in a more compassionate and understanding manner. By acknowledging and validating their feelings, we create a safe space for open and meaningful communication.

Cultural Sensitivity:

In today's diverse world, it is essential to be culturally sensitive when communicating. Different cultures have unique communication styles, customs, and expectations. Failing to recognize and respect these differences can lead to misunderstandings, conflicts, and even offense.

One effective strategy for fostering cultural sensitivity is to be open-minded and curious. Instead of making assumptions based on stereotypes, we can approach intercultural communication with a genuine desire to learn and understand. Asking questions and actively seeking cultural knowledge helps bridge the gap between different perspectives and fosters more inclusive and effective communication.

Adapting to Digital Communication:

In an era dominated by digital technology, we must also consider effective communication strategies in virtual settings. With the rise of emails, instant messaging, and video calls, we must adapt our communication style to the digital realm.

When communicating online, clarity and conciseness are crucial. Messages can easily be misinterpreted, so it's essential to express ourselves clearly and explicitly. Avoiding jargon and using simple language will help ensure that our message is received accurately.

Additionally, being mindful of etiquette in digital communication is vital. Practicing good online manners, such as responding promptly, acknowledging messages, and using appropriate language, can go a long way in building trust and rapport in virtual interactions.

Effective communication is a skill that can always be improved. By implementing the strategies discussed in this chapter, you can enhance your communication abilities and foster stronger connections with others. Whether in personal relationships, professional endeavors, or global interactions, the power of effective communication strategies cannot be underestimated. So, let us embark on this journey of growth and connection, nurturing our words, sharpening our listening skills, and embracing empathy as we become more effective communicators in our ever-evolving world.

Importance of Communication in Leadership

Communication is the cornerstone of successful leadership. Throughout history, great leaders from all walks of life have understood the importance of effective communication in inspiring and guiding their followers towards shared goals. Whether it be on the battlefield, in the corporate world, or in community leadership, the ability to communicate effectively sets leaders apart and creates a solid foundation for achieving success. This chapter explores the essential role of communication in leadership, delving into various aspects and strategies that can enhance their effectiveness.

The Power of Words

Words possess the power to shape thoughts, inspire actions, and build connections. A leader's words can act as a catalyst for change, motivate teams, and foster an environment of trust and transparency. However, it is not merely the words themselves that hold this power but the way in which they are delivered. Effective communication relies not only on the content of the message but also on non-verbal cues, tone, and timing. A leader who understands how to leverage the power of words can influence and inspire individuals towards achieving collective goals.

Clear Vision and Direction

One of the primary responsibilities of a leader is to chart a clear course for their team or organization. Without effective communication, this vision may remain unclear, leading to confusion, demotivation, and a lack of direction. By articulating the vision in a compelling and easily understandable manner, leaders can align their team members towards common objectives, ensuring that everyone moves forward on the same path with a shared purpose. Regular and transparent communication about the vision serves to build trust and commitment within the team, fostering an environment where everyone feels valued and part of the bigger picture.

Building Relationships

A strong leader recognizes the value of building and nurturing relationships with team members. Effective communication plays a crucial role in establishing and maintaining these relationships. By actively listening, seeking feedback, and engaging in meaningful conversations, leaders can foster an atmosphere of open dialogue, respect, and empathy. Additionally, communication allows leaders to understand the diverse strengths, weaknesses, and motivations of team members, enabling them to tailor their leadership style to maximize individual and collective performance.

Motivating and Inspiring

Motivation is a key driver of productivity and success. A leader who can effectively communicate can inspire their team to reach new heights of achievement. Motivation involves not just providing encouragement but also empowering individuals through clear communication of expectations, recognition of accomplishments, and fostering an environment where people feel comfortable taking risks and expressing themselves. By tapping into the intrinsic motivations of team members, leaders can create a sense of ownership and shared commitment to the goals at hand.

Conflict Resolution

In any leadership role, conflict is bound to arise. Effective communication serves as a powerful tool in resolving conflicts, ensuring harmony and productivity within a team or organization. Leaders proficient in communication understand that conflict often stems from misunderstandings, miscommunications, or differing perspectives. They actively engage in active listening, seeking to understand the underlying issues and concerns, and work towards finding equitable resolutions. By facilitating open and honest communication, leaders can reduce tension, maintain trust, and transform conflicts into opportunities for growth and collaboration.

Organizational Alignment

Communication is vital in establishing and upholding organizational alignment. By providing regular updates, sharing important information, and fostering transparent channels of communication, leaders can ensure that everyone within the organization is working towards common goals. This alignment helps to eliminate silos, promote collaboration, and ensure that all team members understand how their work fits into the broader objectives of the organization. Effective communication also encourages innovation and creativity, as individuals feel empowered to share their ideas and perspectives, leading to a culture of continuous improvement.

Enhancing Decision Making

Leaders are often faced with complex decisions that can have far-reaching consequences. Effective communication plays a critical role in this process, enabling leaders to gather the necessary information, seek diverse perspectives, and make informed decisions. By effectively communicating their decisions, leaders can gain buy-in from their teams, ensuring that everyone understands and supports the chosen course of action. Open communication channels also allow leaders to seek feedback and adjust their decisions if necessary, fostering a sense of inclusivity and involvement.

Inspiring Trust and Loyalty

Trust and loyalty are invaluable assets in leadership. Effective communication is a fundamental building block in developing trust and loyalty within a team or organization. A leader who communicates honestly, consistently, and openly fosters an environment of trust, where individuals feel safe to express their concerns and opinions. Trust empowers teams to take risks, engage in constructive conflict, and work towards shared goals without fear of judgment or retribution. Furthermore, leaders who communicate with integrity and transparency instill a sense of loyalty among team members, creating a bond grounded in mutual respect and shared values.

Effective communication lies at the heart of successful leadership. It is the glue that holds teams and organizations together, enabling them to overcome challenges and achieve extraordinary results. By understanding the power of their words, articulating a clear vision, building relationships, inspiring and motivating others, resolving conflicts, aligning the organization, enhancing decision-making, and fostering trust and loyalty, leaders can harness the true potential of their teams. As leaders, it is vital to continually hone our communication skills, as they are a powerful tool to shape the future and leave a lasting impact on those we lead.

Active Listening and Empathetic Communication

In this fast-paced and constantly evolving world, effective communication has become increasingly important. We spend a significant portion of our lives engaging in various forms of communication, be it through verbal exchanges, written messages, or body language. Despite this, we often find ourselves falling into the trap of miscommunication, leading to conflicts and misunderstandings. The key to avoiding such pitfalls lies in mastering the art of active listening and empathetic communication.

Section 1: Understanding Active Listening

1.1 The Essence of Active Listening

Active listening is not merely hearing words but rather a conscious effort to comprehend, interpret, and respond to what is being communicated. It requires more than just the use of our ears; it calls for engaging our mind and senses to truly absorb the message being conveyed. By actively listening, we can build rapport, foster meaningful connections, and strengthen relationships with those around us.

1.2 The Core Principles of Active Listening

To become an effective active listener, we must understand and apply the core principles that underpin this skill:

1.2.1 Paying Attention - Giving our undivided attention to the speaker shows them that we value their words and thoughts. By eliminating distractions, maintaining eye contact, and using non-verbal cues, we demonstrate our commitment to understanding their perspective.

1.2.2 Withholding Judgment - Active listening requires setting aside our biases and preconceived notions. We should refrain from interrupting, critiquing, or jumping to conclusions. By withholding judgment until the speaker has finished, we create a safe environment that encourages open and honest communication.

1.2.3 Clarifying and Summarizing - Seeking clarification when needed and summarizing the speaker's points not only helps us understand the message better but also reassures the speaker that we are actively engaged. It reflects our genuine interest in comprehending their perspective accurately.

Section 2: Mastering Active Listening Techniques

2.1 Paraphrasing and Reflecting Feelings

One of the most effective techniques in active listening is paraphrasing, which involves restating the speaker's message in our own words. By summarizing their thoughts, we confirm our understanding and allow the speaker to clarify any misconceptions. Additionally, reflecting their feelings back to them demonstrates empathy and validates their emotions.

For example, if a friend shares their frustration with work, we may respond by saying, "So, you're feeling overwhelmed and underappreciated by your workload. Is that correct?" This not only conveys that we understand their emotions but also shows that we are actively tuned into their concerns.

2.2 Asking Open-Ended Questions

Open-ended questions are a powerful tool to encourage the speaker to elaborate on their thoughts and feelings. Rather than relying on one-word responses, these questions prompt deeper reflection, allowing for a more fruitful and meaningful conversation. By asking open-ended questions, we demonstrate our interest in their perspective and encourage them to share more.

For example, instead of asking, "Did you enjoy the movie?" we can pose an open-ended question like, "What aspects of the movie resonated with you, and why?" This invites the speaker to delve into their opinions and provides them with an opportunity to express their thoughts freely.

Section 3: Empathetic Communication

3.1 The Importance of Empathy

Empathy lies at the very heart of effective and meaningful communication. It involves the ability to understand and share the emotions of another person. By practicing empathy, we validate the speaker's feelings, foster trust, and establish a deeper connection. Empathy is particularly crucial in sensitive or emotionally charged conversations.

3.2 Developing Empathy

True empathy goes beyond merely recognizing and acknowledging another person's emotions; it involves actively putting ourselves in their shoes. To develop empathy, we must:

3.2.1 Practice Active Listening - As mentioned earlier, active listening is inseparable from empathy. By fully understanding the speaker's message and reflecting their feelings, we demonstrate that we genuinely care and are invested in their experience.

3.2.2 Cultivate Emotional Intelligence - Emotional intelligence entails recognizing and managing our own emotions as well as understanding those of others. By improving our emotional intelligence, we become more attuned to the feelings of those we interact with, enabling us to respond with greater empathy and sensitivity.

3.2.3 Non-Verbal Communication - Non-verbal cues such as facial expressions, body language, and tone of voice convey a wealth of information beyond words. Empathetic individuals pay careful attention to these cues and adjust their responses accordingly to match the emotional context.

Active listening and empathetic communication are indispensable tools in our personal and professional lives. By honing our active listening skills and practicing empathy, we create an environment of understanding, empathy, and respect. Cultivating these abilities allows us to build deeper connections, resolve conflicts more effectively, and foster harmonious relationships. With dedication and practice, anyone can master the art of active listening and empathetic communication, unlocking the true potential of interpersonal communication.

Giving and Receiving Constructive Feedback

We live in a world of constant communication. From the moment we wake up to the time we fall asleep, we are bombarded with messages, whether it is through social media, email, or face-to-face interactions. In this interconnected world, the ability to give and receive constructive feedback becomes paramount. Whether you're a student, a professional, or a friend, knowing how to provide feedback effectively and receive it graciously is a skill that can greatly enhance your personal and professional relationships. This chapter aims to explore the art of giving and receiving constructive feedback, uncover common pitfalls, and provide actionable strategies to improve your feedback skills.

The Power of Constructive Feedback

Constructive feedback is a powerful tool that can drive growth, learning, and improvement. When delivered appropriately, it can motivate individuals to strive for excellence, enhance their skills, and achieve their goals. On the flip side, receiving feedback opens doors for self-awareness, improvement, and personal development. However, the challenge lies in delivering feedback in a way that is empathetic, honest, and constructive. Let's dive into some key principles to consider when giving feedback.

Principle 1: Be Specific and Descriptive

The first principle of giving constructive feedback is to be specific and descriptive. Vague feedback often confuses the recipient and fails to provide them with actionable steps for improvement. Instead of saying, "You're not meeting expectations," try something like, "I noticed that you missed three important details in your report. Can you please review them and make the necessary corrections?"

Descriptive feedback enables the recipient to understand the context and areas for improvement clearly. It also avoids generalizations that may hinder growth and development.

Principle 2: Focus on Behavior, Not Personality

One critical aspect of constructive feedback is to focus on behavior rather than personality. Feedback should be directed towards specific actions or outcomes rather than attacking an individual's character or traits. For example, saying, "You're always so lazy," is not constructive and might cause unnecessary conflict. However, saying, "I noticed that you missed the deadline on two occasions. Is there anything that we can do to ensure timeliness in the future?" provides an opportunity for reflection and improvement without attacking the person's character.

Principle 3: Balance Positive and Negative Feedback

An effective means of giving constructive feedback is to strike a balance between positive and negative feedback. Humans naturally crave recognition and positive reinforcement. Therefore, providing positive feedback alongside constructive criticism can motivate individuals and boost their confidence. Imagine receiving feedback that highlights both your strengths and areas for growth. It would encourage you to continue excelling while working on your weaknesses.

However, be cautious about insincere or excessive positive feedback, as it may undermine the credibility of your constructive criticism. Striving for an earnest balance will ensure that the recipient feels acknowledged and empowered to improve.

Principle 4: Maintain a Growth Mindset

It is crucial to maintain a growth mindset when giving constructive feedback. A growth mindset means believing that people can improve and develop their abilities through effort, practice, and learning from mistakes. By adopting a growth mindset, we can approach feedback conversations as opportunities for growth and development, rather than seeing them as personal attacks. This mindset shift encourages dialogue, open-mindedness, and fosters a culture of continuous improvement.

Principle 5: Use the "Sandwich Method"

The "sandwich method" is a popular technique for giving constructive feedback. It involves surrounding the negative feedback with positive feedback, resembling a sandwich. Start by providing positive feedback to establish rapport and create a safe space. Next, introduce the improvement areas gently but specifically. Finally, end the conversation on a positive note, reaffirming the person's strengths and offering support.

For example, when providing feedback on a colleague's presentation, start with something positive like, "Your presentation had excellent visuals and a powerful opening." Then, address the improvement areas while being specific: "However, I noticed a few instances where you stumbled and lost track of your main points." Finally, conclude with encouragement and support: "I am confident that with some practice, you will deliver exceptional presentations in the future!"

Receiving Constructive Feedback Gracefully

While learning how to give constructive feedback is essential, it is equally important to receive feedback gracefully. Receiving feedback can be challenging, as it may trigger feelings of defensiveness or hurt. However, viewing feedback as an opportunity for growth enriches our personal and professional lives. Let's dive into strategies to receive constructive feedback graciously and maximize its potential.

Strategy 1: Adopt an Open Mind

The first strategy in receiving constructive feedback gracefully is to adopt an open mind. It is natural to feel defensive when receiving feedback, especially if it challenges our self-perception or highlights areas for improvement. However, by approaching feedback with an open mind, we set the stage for personal growth and development. Avoid immediately dismissing or rejecting feedback; instead, take a moment to reflect on it and consider the potential opportunities for improvement it may offer.

Strategy 2: Seek Clarification

When receiving feedback, seeking clarification is crucial for a better understanding of the given insights. If you feel unsure or confused about any aspect of the feedback, do not hesitate to ask for clarifications or examples. Active listening, combined with seeking clarification, fosters a deeper understanding of the feedback and enables you to identify concrete steps for improvement.

Strategy 3: Separate Feedback from Self-Worth

To receive constructive feedback gracefully, it is essential to separate the feedback from your self-worth. Remember that feedback is not a personal attack but rather an opportunity for growth. Understand that receiving feedback does not diminish your value or potential; rather, it provides insights for improvement. By separating the feedback from your identity, you empower yourself to embrace personal growth and development.

Strategy 4: Reflect and Analyze

After receiving constructive feedback, take the time to reflect and analyze the insights. Consider which parts resonate with you and align with your goals. Reflecting on feedback helps you identify patterns, weaknesses, and strengths, enabling you to create a clear roadmap for improvement. Engaging in self-reflection also demonstrates your commitment to personal growth and motivates you to capitalize on the feedback received.

Giving and receiving constructive feedback is an essential aspect of personal growth and professional development. It involves careful consideration of words, empathy, and an open mindset. By following the principles of being specific, focusing on behavior, balancing positive and negative feedback, maintaining a growth mindset, and using the "sandwich method," you can deliver feedback that is both actionable and supportive. Similarly, adopting an open mind, seeking clarification, separating feedback from self-worth, and reflecting on feedback allows you to receive constructive criticism gracefully, fostering personal growth and improvement. By mastering the art of giving and receiving feedback, you can nurture strong relationships, fuel growth, and achieve your aspirations.

Public Speaking and Influencing Skills

In today's fast-paced and interconnected world, the ability to effectively communicate and influence others is more important than ever. Whether you're a CEO, a politician, a teacher, or simply engaging in everyday conversations, the power to speak confidently and persuade others is a skill that can significantly impact your personal and professional life. This chapter delves into the art of public speaking and the secrets behind mastering the art of influencing others.

The Importance of Effective Public Speaking:

Public speaking is an essential skill that allows individuals to communicate their ideas, share knowledge, and inspire others. It goes beyond simply conveying information; it aims to captivate, engage, and motivate the audience. Mastering this skill can open doors to numerous opportunities, boosting career prospects and personal growth.

1. Building Confidence:

One of the key elements of public speaking is building confidence. The fear of speaking in public is one of the most common phobias among individuals. However, by conquering this fear and developing confidence in your abilities, you unlock a wealth of possibilities.

Confidence helps you project authority, credibility, and competence, making your message more influential.

2. Effective Communication:

Public speaking encompasses not only verbal communication but also non-verbal cues such as body language, tone of voice, and facial expressions. Being aware of these aspects allows you to communicate your message with clarity and impact. Paying attention to your body language ensures that your words, gestures, and expressions are aligned, increasing your credibility and persuasiveness.

Components of Effective Public Speaking:

1. Preparation:

Effective speakers understand the importance of preparation. This involves thoroughly researching the topic, organizing thoughts, and creating a logical structure for the presentation. Adequate preparation ensures coherence, addresses potential questions, and enhances the overall impact of your speech.

2. Knowing Your Audience:

Understanding your audience is crucial in tailoring your message to resonate with them. Analyze their demographics, interests, and motivations to align your speech with their needs and expectations. This knowledge empowers you to connect with the audience on a deeper level and deliver a memorable presentation.

3. Captivating Opening:

The first few moments of a speech can make or break the audience's engagement. A captivating opening grabs attention and sets the tone for the entire talk. Utilize storytelling techniques, pose thought-provoking questions, or share intriguing statistics to instantly capture the audience's interest.

4. Engaging Delivery:

Delivering a speech with enthusiasm and dynamic energy keeps the audience engaged. Vary your tone, pace, and volume to emphasize key points and maintain the audience's interest. Incorporate visual aids such as slides, props, or videos to illustrate complex concepts and enhance understanding.

Mastering the Art of Influence:

Public speaking and influencing skills go hand in hand. Effective persuasion involves not just delivering an impactful speech but also understanding how to influence others' beliefs, decisions, and actions. Here are techniques that can significantly enhance your influencing abilities:

1. Establishing Credibility:

Before attempting to influence others, establish your credibility. People are more likely to follow someone they perceive as knowledgeable, trustworthy, and authentic. Share relevant experiences, expertise, or credentials to demonstrate your expertise and build rapport with your audience.

2. Use Emotional Appeal:

Emotions often play a significant role in decision-making. Tapping into the emotions of your audience can make your message more compelling and persuasive. By connecting your topic to their values, desires, or fears, you can foster an emotional bond that drives them to act.

3. Developing Strong Arguments:

Effective persuasion requires presenting compelling arguments. Support your claims with evidence, statistics, or real-life examples that resonate with your audience. Anticipate counterarguments and address them proactively, reinforcing the credibility of your position.

4. Active Listening and Empathy:

Influencing others is not solely about talking; it also involves active listening and empathy. Understanding the concerns, needs, and perspectives of others allows you to tailor your message accordingly. Listening attentively, acknowledging their opinions, and responding empathetically fosters trust and receptivity.

Public speaking and influencing skills are invaluable assets for personal and professional growth. They empower individuals to confidently convey ideas, inspire others, and influence positive change. By mastering the art of public speaking and understanding the intricacies of influence, you can open doors to countless opportunities and make a lasting impact on those around you. Continual practice, self-reflection, and an openness to learning are crucial to becoming a powerful communicator and influencer.

Chapter 6: Leading through Change and Adversity

In today's fast-paced and ever-evolving world, change and adversity have become part and parcel of our lives. Whether it's navigating through economic downturns, technological disruptions, or personal challenges, leaders must possess the ability to adapt and navigate their teams through uncertain times. In this chapter, we delve deep into the art of leading through change and adversity, exploring essential strategies and insights that will help leaders excel in the face of adversity and bring about positive transformation.

Navigating the Change Landscape:

Change is not a linear process; it's often an intricate maze that requires finesse and agility to navigate successfully. As a leader, understanding the different stages of change can help you guide your team through the transformational journey effectively.

The first stage is the recognition of the need for change. Whether it's due to external factors or internal opportunities, recognizing the need for change sets the groundwork for transformation. As a leader, your role is to communicate this need with clarity, ensuring your team understands the rationale behind it and its potential benefits.

The next stage involves planning and preparation. This phase requires meticulous attention to detail, as creating a robust plan is crucial for a smooth transition. Prioritize open communication with your team, involving them in the planning process and gathering their valuable insights. By doing so, you foster a shared sense of ownership, making individuals more receptive to change.

Implementing Change:

Implementing change is often the most challenging phase for leaders. It requires a delicate balance of firmness and flexibility to manage resistance effectively. Start by establishing clear goals and expectations, ensuring everyone is aligned with the desired outcomes. Regularly communicate progress, address any concerns, and celebrate small victories along the way. By creating a positive and supportive environment, you pave the way for your team's acceptance and commitment to the change process.

During this phase, leaders must be empathetic and understanding. Resistance to change is natural and can stem from fear, uncertainty, or discomfort. Take the time to listen to your team members' concerns, provide reassurance, and offer support where needed. By demonstrating trust and transparency, you can build stronger relationships, fostering a culture of resilience and adaptability.

Leading through Adversity:

Adversity comes in many forms - from personal setbacks to external challenges. Leaders must be equipped with the skills and mindset necessary to navigate these difficult periods.

During times of adversity, communication becomes paramount. Transparency is key, as it allows you to provide updates, address concerns, and rally your team's support. Regularly check in with your team members individually, offering them a safe space to share their emotions and concerns. Active listening and compassion go a long way in building trust and solidarity, motivating individuals to work collectively towards overcoming obstacles.

Moreover, leaders must lead by example. During challenging times, your team looks to you for guidance and inspiration. Demonstrating resilience and optimism can create a contagious effect, instilling confidence and determination within your team. Emphasize the importance of a growth mindset and encourage everyone to learn and grow from setbacks, using them as opportunities for personal and professional development.

Building a Supportive Culture:

To effectively lead through change and adversity, leaders must foster a supportive culture that empowers individuals to embrace challenges and drive continuous improvement.

Firstly, promote learning and development within your team. Encourage individuals to expand their skill sets, invest in training programs, and share their knowledge with one another. By cultivating a culture of continuous learning, you equip your team with the tools and capabilities needed to adapt to new circumstances confidently.

Secondly, celebrate resilience and collaboration. Recognize and reward your team members' efforts in navigating difficult situations, reinforcing the importance of tenacity and teamwork. Acknowledge the strengths and diversity within your team, leveraging them to drive innovation and creativity even during trying times.

Lastly, embrace feedback and maintain an open-door policy. Encourage constructive criticism and suggestions from your team members, fostering a culture of trust and continuous improvement. Actively seek feedback from those you lead and be receptive to change and adaptation yourself.

Leading through change and adversity is a complex and dynamic process that tests the mettle of even the most experienced leaders. By understanding the stages of change, implementing effective strategies, and fostering a supportive culture, leaders can navigate their teams through uncertain times with confidence and resilience. The ability to adapt, communicate effectively, and inspire others in the face of adversity distinguishes exceptional leaders. Remember, great leaders are not defined by how they handle success but by how they lead during times of change and adversity.

Embracing Change as a Leader

Change is the only constant in life; a proverb that rings true across all aspects of our existence, including the realm of leadership. In today's fast-paced and ever-evolving world, leaders who resist or fear change will find themselves left behind, while those who embrace and harness its power will thrive. In this chapter, we will explore the importance of embracing change as a leader, the challenges it poses, and how to navigate through these uncertainties to create a positive impact on your organization and team.

Understanding the Need for Change

Before delving into the significance of embracing change, it is imperative to comprehend why change is necessary and inevitable. The business landscape is in a constant state of flux due to globalization, advancements in technology, shifting market trends, and ever-changing customer expectations. These external factors impose challenges on organizations and demand nimble leaders who can adapt and respond effectively to the changing environment.

Additionally, change is essential for growth and innovation. By encouraging and embracing change, leaders create an environment where creativity flourishes, new ideas emerge, and organizations remain agile and relevant. It is through change that great achievements are made, and new possibilities emerge.

Embracing Change as a Mindset

To effectively embrace change, leaders must cultivate the right mindset. It begins with accepting that change is an opportunity rather than a threat. By viewing change positively, leaders can inspire their teams to adapt, grow, and thrive amidst uncertainty.

A mindset of resilience is also necessary. Change often brings unforeseen obstacles and setbacks. Leaders must prepare themselves and their teams to persevere through such challenges, maintaining a sense of determination and positivity even in the face of adversity.

Moreover, a growth mindset is vital in embracing change. Recognizing that every change presents opportunities for learning and personal development, leaders who consistently seek self-improvement foster a culture that inspires continuous growth within their teams.

Overcoming Resistance to Change

Despite the obvious benefits, change is often met with resistance, both from individuals and within organizations. As leaders, it is crucial to acknowledge and address this resistance proactively. By promoting open communication and transparent dialogue, leaders can help alleviate fears, concerns, and uncertainties associated with change.

Effective change management involves clearly articulating the vision and rationale behind the change, outlining the potential benefits it will bring to individuals and the organization as a whole. Engaging employees in discussions and actively seeking their input cultivates a sense of ownership and empowers them to participate in the change process.

Leaders must also provide support and resources to help individuals navigate through the change. By offering training, mentoring, and allocating sufficient time for adaptation, leaders can alleviate anxiety and enhance the probability of a successful transition.

Communication and Collaboration

In times of change, effective communication and collaboration become paramount. Leaders should employ a proactive approach, ensuring that all relevant stakeholders are kept well-informed throughout the process. Transparent communication builds trust, manages expectations, and minimizes uncertainties, thus promoting a smoother transition.

Furthermore, collaboration is instrumental in embracing change successfully. As a leader, fostering a collaborative culture encourages teamwork, idea-sharing, and collective problem-solving. When diverse perspectives are acknowledged and valued, individuals feel a sense of ownership, leading to a greater commitment to change initiatives.

Promotion of Innovation and Creativity

Embracing change provides a fertile ground for innovation and creativity to thrive. Leaders must create an environment that fosters and rewards innovation, empowering their teams to think differently and take risks. By encouraging experimentation and learning from failures, leaders inspire their teams to continuously innovate and adapt to change.

Moreover, leaders should lead by example and actively participate in the creative process. By challenging traditional thinking, questioning the status quo, and taking calculated risks themselves, leaders instill a culture of innovation that permeates throughout the organization.

Adapting to Technological Advancements

Technological advancements have revolutionized the way we live and work. As a leader, embracing technological change is essential for staying competitive and relevant. Leveraging technology enables leaders to streamline processes, enhance productivity, and provide new solutions to customer needs.

However, adapting to technological advancements is not without its challenges. Leaders must remain vigilant to the risks associated with technology, such as cybersecurity threats and ethical dilemmas. Striking a balance between embracing technology and ensuring ethical practices is crucial for leaders to navigate through this digital era successfully.

Managing Resistance and Overcoming Challenges

While embracing change is crucial for growth and success, it is not without its share of challenges. Resistance to change, fear of the unknown, and the tendency to revert to established routines can hinder progress. As a leader, it is essential to be prepared to face these challenges head-on.

Recognizing that change takes time and persistence is vital. Leaders must be patient, persistent, and tenacious when leading their teams through change. By offering continuous support, celebrating small successes, and providing regular feedback, leaders can help individuals overcome resistance and adapt to the new normal.

Additionally, leaders must be flexible and adaptable in their approach. The ability to pivot and respond swiftly to unexpected circumstances is crucial in navigating through change successfully. By continuously assessing and adjusting strategies, leaders can proactively address any emerging challenges and cater to the evolving needs of their teams and organizations.

The Power of Continuous Learning

In embracing change as a leader, one must recognize the power of continuous learning. Change presents opportunities for personal growth, and leaders should seize these occasions to enhance their knowledge and skills.

Leaders must remain curious, seeking out new experiences and perspectives. Embracing change requires a strong sense of self-awareness and the ability to reflect on one's own strengths and areas for improvement. By seeking feedback, engaging in self-reflection, and actively pursuing professional development opportunities, leaders can continue evolving and adapting to the ever-changing landscape of leadership.

As leaders, embracing change is not just an option but a necessity. By cultivating a growth mindset, effectively managing resistance, promoting open communication and collaboration, fostering innovation and creativity, and continuously learning and growing, leaders can navigate through the uncertainties of change and create positive transformations within their organizations.

Embracing change is not a one-time occurrence but an ongoing journey. By committing to embracing change as a leader, you not only position yourself and your organization for success but also inspire and empower others to thrive in an ever-changing world. So, take charge, embrace change, and create a future where possibilities are limitless.

Strategies for Navigating Uncertainty

In today's fast-paced and ever-changing world, uncertainty has become a constant companion. From economic volatility to global pandemics, individuals and organizations alike find themselves grappling with an uncertain future. While we cannot completely eliminate uncertainty from our lives, we can develop strategies to navigate this unpredictable terrain successfully. In this chapter, we explore various tactics and approaches that will empower you to embrace uncertainty, adapt to change, and thrive in the face of ambiguity.

Section 1: Embracing Uncertainty

In our quest for security and stability, our natural tendency is to resist uncertainty. However, true growth and innovation lie in embracing ambiguity rather than shying away from it. Uncertainty offers opportunities for creativity, learning, and transformation. By shifting our mindset and embracing uncertainty as a natural part of life, we can effectively handle the unpredictable.

1.1 Developing Resilience:

Resilience is the ability to bounce back from challenges and adapt to new circumstances. Building resilience helps us navigate uncertainty with a positive mindset. Practices such as mindfulness meditation, regular exercise, and maintaining a strong support network can enhance our ability to bounce back from setbacks and face the unknown with confidence.

1.2 Cultivating a Growth Mindset:

A growth mindset involves perceiving challenges and failures as opportunities for learning and personal development. By reframing uncertainty as a chance to grow and expand our skills, we can maintain a positive outlook and better navigate ambiguity. Embracing a growth mindset encourages us to experiment, take calculated risks, and continually seek improvement.

Section 2: Adapting to Change

Change is an integral part of life, and our ability to adapt directly impacts our success in uncertain circumstances. By developing strategies to embrace and leverage change, we can effectively navigate through unchartered territory.

2.1 Anticipating Change:

While some changes are unexpected, others can be predicted to some extent. Monitoring trends, staying informed about technological advancements, and conducting scenario planning are effective ways to anticipate change. By recognizing potential disruptions in advance, we can proactively respond to them and minimize their impact on our lives and organizations.

2.2 Building Flexibility:

Flexibility is the cornerstone of adaptability. Being open to new ideas, perspectives, and approaches allows us to respond promptly and effectively to change. To build flexibility, we must challenge our preconceived notions, actively seek diverse experiences, and embrace a growth mindset. Additionally, cultivating a strong network of collaborators and mentors can provide invaluable support and guidance during uncertain times.

Section 3: Thriving in Ambiguity

To truly thrive in uncertainty, we must not only embrace it but also make the most of the ambiguous nature of our situations. This section explores strategies to help us leverage the potential of ambiguity to our advantage.

3.1 Embracing Ambiguity as an Opportunity:

Rather than viewing ambiguity as a threat, we can choose to see it as an opportunity for innovation and growth. Cultivating a mindset that views ambiguity as a blank canvas allows us to explore new possibilities and take advantage of emerging trends. Encouraging curiosity and embracing experimentation becomes second nature when we approach ambiguity with an open mind.

3.2 Building Adaptive Capabilities:

Being adaptable is crucial in embracing ambiguity. Developing skills such as critical thinking, problem-solving, and emotional intelligence equips us to thrive in ambiguous situations. Organizations can foster a culture that encourages flexibility, creativity, and collaboration, empowering employees to navigate uncertainty collectively.

3.3 Emphasizing Continuous Learning:

In uncertain times, the ability to learn quickly and continuously is paramount. Embracing a growth mindset and actively seeking out opportunities for learning and personal development are essential strategies to navigate ambiguity successfully. Engaging in lifelong learning allows us to stay relevant, adapt to new circumstances, and find innovative solutions to complex problems.

Navigating uncertainty is an indispensable skill in today's rapidly changing world. By embracing uncertainty, adapting to change, and thriving in ambiguity, we can transform uncertainty from a hindrance into a catalyst for growth and innovation. The strategies discussed in this chapter offer a roadmap to embracing the unknown with resilience, agility, and confidence. Remember, uncertainty is not a barrier; it is an invitation to explore new horizons and unlock our true potential.

Leading Teams during Crisis

In times of crisis, effective leadership is essential to guide teams through the storm and ensure their survival. It is during these challenging moments that the true mettle of a leader is tested. The ability to inspire, engage, and unite team members in the face of adversity is paramount for reaching successful outcomes. This chapter explores the key attributes and strategies required to lead teams during times of crisis, emphasizing the importance of empathy, decisiveness, and adaptability.

1. The Role of the Leader in Crisis Management:

During a crisis, the leader shoulders the responsibility of steering the team towards stability and success. It is imperative for leaders to assume a proactive stance in crisis management, demonstrating resilience and providing direction to their team members. By maintaining a calm and composed demeanor, leaders can instill a sense of confidence and trust in their teams, encouraging them to remain focused and motivated despite the challenges they face.

2. Establishing a Clear Vision:

In times of crisis, it is crucial for leaders to establish a clear vision and communicate it effectively to their team members. A shared understanding of objectives and direction creates a sense of purpose, driving team members to work towards a common goal. By providing clarity and setting achievable targets, leaders enable their teams to navigate through uncertainty and work towards a better future.

3. Building Trust and Empathy:

Trust is the bedrock upon which effective leadership stands, and crises provide a unique opportunity for leaders to cultivate this essential element. By demonstrating empathy, actively listening, and responding to the emotional needs of their team members, leaders can foster a culture of trust and empathy within the team. This creates an environment where individuals feel safe to be vulnerable, share their concerns, and collaboratively work towards solutions.

4. Effective Communication:

During a crisis, communication becomes even more critical as team members seek reassurance, clarity, and guidance. Leaders must adopt an open and transparent communication style, ensuring that information flows smoothly and promptly within the team. Regular updates, team briefings, and clear expectations help alleviate anxiety, enhance collaboration, and maintain a motivated and engaged team.

5. Decisiveness and Flexibility:

Crises often require leaders to make swift decisions in the face of ambiguity and uncertainty. The ability to assess situations, analyze data, and make sound judgments in a timely manner is a hallmark of effective leadership during trying times. Additionally, leaders must be flexible and adaptable, as a crisis may necessitate altering plans, changing strategies, or pivoting to new approaches. Embracing innovation and encouraging experimentation can help teams adapt to evolving circumstances and uncover new opportunities amid crisis.

6. Empowering and Supporting the Team:

In times of crisis, leaders must empower their team members to take ownership of their roles and responsibilities. Encouraging autonomy not only boosts morale but also helps team members develop their problem-solving skills, enabling them to contribute meaningfully to the organization's recovery. Leaders should provide the necessary support, resources, and guidance required for their teams to navigate the challenges they face, fostering a sense of unity and shared accountability.

7. Leading by Example:

Exemplary leadership sets an inspiring tone and provides a roadmap for team members to follow. During a crisis, leaders must be role models, embodying the values, behaviors, and attitudes they expect from their team. By maintaining a positive outlook, practicing resilience, and remaining composed in the face of adversity, leaders demonstrate the strength and determination required to overcome challenges. This, in turn, motivates and encourages team members to emulate these qualities, helping them navigate through the crisis with greater confidence.

8. Implementing Continuous Learning:

Every crisis carries valuable lessons that can shape future decision-making and strengthen the team's resilience. Leaders should create an environment that encourages continuous learning and improvement, fostering a growth mindset within the team. Post-crisis reflection, analysis, and knowledge sharing sessions enable team members to identify areas for improvement, implement necessary changes, and build a stronger foundation to face future challenges.

Leading teams during a crisis demands exceptional leadership qualities and a deep understanding of the unique dynamics that emerge during such challenging times. By establishing a clear vision, building trust and empathy, communicating effectively, making decisive yet flexible decisions, empowering team members, and setting an example, leaders can successfully guide their teams through the storm. The lessons learned from leading teams through crisis not only strengthen an organization's resilience but also provide invaluable personal growth opportunities for both leaders and their teams.

Transforming Challenges into Opportunities

Life is a journey, filled with moments that test our resilience and push us to our limits. Challenges come in different shapes and sizes, and they can manifest in various aspects of our lives - be it personal, professional, or spiritual. However, it is important to remember that challenges are not meant to break us but to make us stronger. In this chapter, we explore the transformative power of challenges and how we can harness them to unlock hidden opportunities.

Understanding Challenges

Challenges are inevitable in life; they are a natural part of the human experience. They emerge unexpectedly and can blindside us, leaving us feeling overwhelmed and uncertain about our abilities. It is during these moments that we must remind ourselves that challenges are not obstacles meant to stop us in our tracks but rather opportunities for growth and self-discovery.

Challenges allow us to confront our fears, test our limits, and broaden our understanding of the world. They force us out of our comfort zones and propel us towards self-improvement. While it is tempting to resist and avoid challenges, embracing them head-on is the key to unlocking their hidden potential.

Shifting Perspectives: From Problems to Opportunities

One of the most crucial aspects of transforming challenges into opportunities lies in our ability to shift our perspective. Oftentimes, challenges are perceived as problems that hinder our progress and diminish our happiness. However, by reframing our mindset and viewing challenges as opportunities for growth and learning, we can transform how we approach and overcome them.

Adopting a growth mindset allows us to see that every challenge is an opportunity in disguise. Recognizing that setbacks and obstacles are not permanent roadblocks but temporary detours can help us navigate through difficulties. When we embrace challenges as opportunities, we open ourselves up to new possibilities and future achievements.

Adapting to Change

Change is one of the fundamental reasons why challenges arise in our lives. Whether it is a sudden job loss, a career transition, or the end of a relationship, change can be unsettling and cause immense discomfort. However, it is crucial to remember that change is the catalyst for personal growth and transformation.

By embracing change and viewing it as an opportunity for self-reflection and reinvention, we can navigate the challenges that come along with it. Instead of resisting change, we must embrace it as a chance to reassess our goals, redefine our priorities, and discover new paths. Change may be intimidating, but it often holds the key to unlocking hidden potentials within ourselves.

Resilience and Perseverance

Resilience and perseverance are powerful qualities that enable us to face challenges head-on. These characteristics harness our inner strength and fortitude, allowing us to withstand hardships and continue moving forward despite setbacks.

Resilience is the ability to bounce back from adversity, to adapt and recover. It helps us regain our balance and focus on finding solutions rather than dwelling on problems. Building resilience requires patience and self-compassion. We must learn to nurture ourselves during difficult times, practicing self-care and seeking support when needed.

Perseverance, on the other hand, is the determination to persist despite obstacles and setbacks. It is the driving force that fuels our journey towards success. Perseverance requires a strong belief in ourselves and our ability to overcome challenges. When we persevere, we develop a resilience that not only helps us face the current challenge but also prepares us for future ones.

Embracing Growth through Vulnerability

Vulnerability is often viewed as a weakness, but in reality, it is a gateway to growth and transformation. By allowing ourselves to be vulnerable, we open the door to new experiences, connections, and opportunities.

When faced with challenges, it is important to embrace vulnerability and be willing to ask for help. Seeking support from others not only lightens the burden but also allows us to tap into a collective wisdom that may provide us with new perspectives and solutions.

Moreover, vulnerability fosters authenticity and self-acceptance. It enables us to acknowledge our limitations and embrace our imperfections without judgment. By accepting our vulnerabilities, we can grow into stronger and more resilient individuals.

Challenges are an integral part of the human experience, and how we perceive and approach them determines our ability to transform them into opportunities for growth and self-discovery. Shifting our perspective, embracing change, cultivating resilience and perseverance, and embracing vulnerability are all essential steps in this transformation process.

Instead of succumbing to the weight of our challenges, let us view them as stepping stones on our journey towards personal and professional development. By harnessing the transformative power of challenges, we can uncover hidden opportunities, unlock our potential, and ultimately, lead a fulfilling and purposeful life.

Chapter 7: Leveraging Diversity and Inclusion

In today's globalized world, the power of diversity and inclusion cannot be overstated. Organizations that embrace and leverage diversity are often at the forefront of innovation, creativity, and success. In this chapter, we will explore the significance of diversity and inclusion for businesses, strategies for fostering an inclusive workplace, and the benefits that come from managing diversity effectively.

Understanding Diversity

Diversity encompasses all the ways in which individuals differ from each other. It includes visible dimensions such as race, ethnicity, gender, age, and physical abilities, but also encompasses less visible dimensions like sexual orientation, religious beliefs, education level, and work experience. To truly leverage diversity, it is essential to recognize and value the multitude of ways people differ in order to create an inclusive environment.

The Importance of Inclusion

While diversity refers to the mix of individuals within an organization, inclusion focuses on ensuring that each individual feels valued and included, regardless of their differences. Inclusion is about creating an environment where all employees have a sense of belonging, respect, and equal access to opportunities. Without inclusion, diversity efforts can fall short, resulting in a fragmented workforce and missed opportunities for growth.

Creating an Inclusive Workplace

Developing a truly inclusive workplace requires intentional effort and a commitment from all levels of the organization. Here are some strategies to foster inclusivity:

1. Leadership Commitment: Building an inclusive workplace starts with leadership commitment. When leaders understand the value of diversity and commit to fostering inclusion, it sets the tone for the entire organization. Leaders should take responsibility for championing diversity and inclusion initiatives and ensure they are integrated into the company's values, policies, and practices.

2. Diverse Recruitment and Hiring Practices: To create a diverse workforce, organizations must implement recruitment and hiring practices that attract candidates from various backgrounds. This includes reviewing job descriptions for bias, using diverse recruitment sources, and implementing blind resume screening processes to mitigate unconscious biases.

3. Cultural Competence Training: Cultural competence training helps employees understand and appreciate different cultures, perspectives, and communication styles. It promotes empathy and helps avoid misunderstandings, fostering a more inclusive and respectful workplace. Providing learning opportunities to employees on topics such as unconscious bias, microaggressions, and cultural awareness can significantly enhance inclusivity.

4. Employee Resource Groups: Employee resource groups (ERGs) are voluntary, employee-led groups that bring together individuals with shared characteristics or interests. ERGs provide a platform for employees to connect, support, and mentor each other, ultimately promoting inclusivity throughout the organization. These groups contribute to fostering a sense of belonging while also acting as an information-sharing network to address challenges faced by underrepresented groups.

5. Mentorship and Sponsorship Programs: Mentorship and sponsorship programs are effective tools for breaking down barriers and promoting inclusivity. These programs connect individuals from diverse backgrounds with experienced leaders who can provide guidance, career development, and opportunities for advancement. By fostering relationships between employees of different backgrounds, these programs help bridge gaps and create a supportive environment.

Benefits of Managing Diversity Effectively

When an organization successfully manages diversity and inclusion, it can reap numerous benefits that contribute to its overall success. Some key benefits include:

1. Increased Innovation: A diverse workforce brings together different perspectives, experiences, and ideas. This diversity of thought fuels innovation and creativity, leading to the development of unique products, services, and solutions. Organizations that embrace diversity and inclusion tend to have a competitive edge in the market by being more adaptable and responsive to changing customer needs.

2. Enhanced Employee Engagement and Retention: Inclusive workplaces foster a sense of belonging and loyalty, leading to higher employee engagement and retention rates. When employees feel valued and respected for their unique contributions, they are more likely to be committed to the organization, resulting in higher productivity and reduced turnover.

3. Expanded Market Reach: Embracing diversity not only facilitates innovation but also helps organizations tap into new markets. When a company's workforce reflects the diversity of its customers, it gains better insights into diverse markets, leading to improved customer understanding, loyalty, and increased market share.

4. Improved Problem-Solving and Decision-Making: Diverse teams bring together a variety of perspectives and experiences, leading to more robust problem-solving and better decision-making. Different viewpoints challenge assumptions and biases, leading to more comprehensive and innovative solutions.

5. Enhanced Reputation and Brand Image: Organizations that prioritize diversity and inclusion demonstrate their commitment to social responsibility and equality. This, in turn, enhances their reputation and brand image, making them more attractive to prospective employees, clients, and stakeholders.

In a world where diversity is the norm, organizations must embrace and leverage the power of inclusivity. By creating a workplace where individuals feel valued and respected for their unique contributions, organizations can unlock a wealth of benefits such as increased innovation, enhanced employee engagement, expanded market reach, improved problem-solving, and a strong reputation. A diverse and inclusive workforce is not only a strategic advantage but also a reflection of a just and equitable society, paving the way for a brighter future for all.

Understanding the Value of Diversity in Teams

In today's rapidly evolving business landscape, organizations are recognizing the significance of diversity in teams as a key driver of success. The demographics of our society are changing, and with it, the need for businesses to embrace diversity in order to remain competitive. In this chapter, we will delve into the value of diversity in teams, exploring the benefits it brings, the challenges it poses, and the strategies organizations can employ to leverage its advantages.

Why Diversity Matters

Diversity encompasses a wide range of attributes, such as race, gender, age, ethnicity, socioeconomic background, education, and more. It goes beyond mere compliance with equal opportunity legislation; it is about creating an inclusive environment where individuals from all walks of life can thrive. The value of diversity lies in its ability to foster innovation, enhance decision-making, and bridge cultural gaps.

One of the primary benefits of diversity in teams is the diverse range of perspectives it brings. When team members come from different backgrounds, they bring with them unique insights, experiences, and knowledge. This diversity of thought fuels creativity and innovation, enabling organizations to adapt and respond to complex problems more effectively. A homogenous team with limited perspectives may fail to consider alternative solutions, leading to missed opportunities and stunted growth.

Further, diversity improves decision-making by minimizing inherent biases. Research has consistently shown that diverse teams make better decisions compared to homogeneous teams. By including individuals with varying perspectives, backgrounds, and expertise, organizations can reduce the risks of groupthink and increase the likelihood of making informed, well-rounded decisions.

Moreover, diversity in teams helps businesses tap into a more extensive market base. With globalization, organizations are increasingly operating in multicultural and multinational environments. By having diverse teams, businesses can better understand and cater to the needs and desires of diverse customer segments. This not only helps in product and service innovation but also enhances customer engagement and loyalty, leading to improved business performance.

Challenges Associated with Diversity

While the value of diversity is undeniable, it is crucial to acknowledge and address the challenges that may arise. These challenges often stem from unconscious biases, lack of inclusive company culture, and difficulties in managing diverse teams effectively.

One of the primary impediments to harnessing the value of diversity is unconscious bias. We all possess unconscious biases, shaped by societal norms and personal experiences, which influence our judgments and decisions. These biases can lead to preferential treatment or exclusion of certain team members, hindering collaboration and stifling creativity. Overcoming unconscious biases requires raising awareness, providing diversity training, and fostering a culture of inclusivity.

Another challenge is the lack of inclusive company culture. Organizations need to cultivate an environment that celebrates diversity rather than merely tolerating it. Leadership plays a vital role in setting the tone and creating a culture where everyone's contributions are valued and respected. This includes policies and practices that promote diversity and inclusion at all levels, ensuring a safe and supportive space for diverse talents to thrive.

Effective Strategies for Leveraging Diversity

To leverage the full potential of diversity in teams, organizations can adopt various strategies that facilitate collaboration, foster inclusion, and drive innovation.

Firstly, creating diverse teams intentionally is crucial. Organizations need to make conscious efforts to build teams that bring together individuals with different backgrounds, perspectives, and skills. This can be achieved through inclusive recruitment practices, recognizing that diversity goes beyond visible attributes and encompasses cognitive diversity as well.

Next, organizations should invest in diversity training and development programs. These initiatives should focus on raising awareness of unconscious biases, promoting cultural competence, and providing tools to navigate differences effectively. Effective training can help dismantle stereotypes, enhance communication skills, and foster understanding among team members.

Implementing inclusion initiatives is equally important. This can include establishing employee resource groups, mentoring programs, or affinity networks where individuals with similar backgrounds can connect, share experiences, and find support. Inclusion initiatives not only promote a sense of belonging but also provide opportunities for professional growth and networking.

In addition, organizations should create platforms and spaces for open dialogue and collaboration. By encouraging team members to express their thoughts and opinions freely, organizations can tap into the collective intelligence and diverse perspectives of their employees. Open communication fosters trust, respect, and empathy, leading to increased employee engagement and a stronger team dynamic.

Understanding the value of diversity in teams is crucial for organizations seeking to realize their full potential and remain competitive in today's global marketplace. By embracing diversity as a strategic asset, organizations can cultivate an inclusive environment that fosters innovation, enhances decision-making, and taps into diverse market segments. Overcoming the challenges associated with diversity requires an intentional effort to address unconscious biases, foster an inclusive company culture, and implement effective strategies for collaboration. By doing so, organizations can build teams that celebrate differences, drive performance, and shape a better future for all.

Fostering an Inclusive Work Environment

Creating an inclusive work environment is not just a noble pursuit; it is essential for the success and growth of any organization. In today's diverse and globalized world, companies that embrace inclusivity reap numerous benefits, including increased productivity, innovation, and employee satisfaction. However, fostering an inclusive work environment is not a one-time effort but an ongoing journey that requires commitment and a deep understanding of the complex dynamics at play. In this chapter, we will explore the key elements and strategies for creating an inclusive work environment that values diversity, promotes equality, and focuses on the overall well-being of its employees.

Understanding Diversity:

Before delving into the specifics of fostering inclusivity, it is crucial to comprehend the concept of diversity. Diversity extends beyond differences in race, ethnicity, gender, and age. It encompasses a broad range of individual characteristics, experiences, and perspectives that shape our identities and influence how we navigate the world. Embracing diversity means acknowledging and valuing these unique traits to create an environment where everyone feels respected, heard, and empowered to contribute their ideas and talents.

The Importance of Inclusion:

While diversity focuses on representation, inclusion goes a step further by actively engaging and integrating diverse perspectives. Inclusion ensures that all employees feel seen, heard, and valued in the decision-making process and day-to-day operations of the organization. By fostering an inclusive work environment, companies can tap into the full potential of their diverse workforce, leading to improved creativity, problem-solving, and overall organizational performance.

Leadership Commitment:

Creating an inclusive work environment starts at the top. Leadership commitment is essential to set the tone and values of the organization. Leaders must visibly demonstrate their commitment to inclusivity through both words and actions. They should communicate the importance of diversity and inclusion as core values, and ensure all employees understand their role in fostering an inclusive workplace culture. By prioritizing inclusivity, leaders inspire others to follow suit and create a ripple effect throughout the organization.

Building Awareness and Education:

One of the foundational elements of fostering an inclusive work environment is building awareness and providing education on diverse perspectives and experiences. Organizations can organize workshops, training sessions, and guest speakers to educate employees and raise awareness about unconscious bias, microaggressions, and the impact of privilege. These initiatives help employees identify and challenge their own biases, fostering a more inclusive mindset and behavior.

Equitable Policies and Practices:

To create an inclusive work environment, organizations must evaluate their policies and practices through an equity lens. This involves critically examining recruitment and hiring processes, promotion criteria, compensation structures, and performance evaluations to ensure they are unbiased and free from discrimination. Removing barriers and promoting equal opportunities for all employees regardless of their backgrounds is crucial for fostering inclusivity.

Empowering Employee Resource Groups:

Employee Resource Groups (ERGs) play a vital role in fostering inclusivity. ERGs are voluntary, employee-led groups formed around shared characteristics or experiences, such as gender, ethnicity, or disability. By empowering these groups, organizations provide employees with a platform to connect, support one another, and advocate for positive change within the organization. ERGs also contribute to organizational decision-making by generating diverse perspectives and innovative ideas.

Promoting Collaboration and Allyship:

Collaboration and allyship are powerful tools in creating an inclusive work environment. Encouraging employees to work collaboratively across teams and departments helps break down silos and fosters a sense of shared understanding and purpose. Furthermore, allyship involves individuals with privilege actively supporting and advancing the voices and rights of underrepresented colleagues. By promoting collaboration and allyship, organizations create a sense of solidarity and collective responsibility for inclusivity.

Mitigating Unconscious Bias:

Unconscious bias refers to the unconscious associations and stereotypes that influence our perceptions and decision-making. It is crucial for organizations to implement strategies to mitigate unconscious bias. This can include blind recruitment processes, where candidate information is anonymized to reduce bias during initial screening. Training programs should also be implemented to raise awareness of unconscious bias and equip employees with the tools to challenge and overcome it.

Empathy and Psychological Safety:

Fostering an inclusive work environment necessitates creating a culture of empathy and psychological safety. Employees should feel comfortable expressing their opinions, sharing their experiences, and taking risks without fear of judgment or reprisal. Building trust and open communication channels is essential for creating an environment where employees feel heard, respected, and supported.

Effective Communication and Feedback:

Effective communication plays a crucial role in fostering an inclusive work environment. Organizations should prioritize transparent communication channels that encourage dialogue, active listening, and open feedback. Communication should be two-way, allowing employees at all levels to share their thoughts, concerns, and ideas. Regular feedback and employee engagement surveys enable organizations to assess their progress and identify areas for improvement.

Creating an inclusive work environment is a multifaceted and ongoing endeavor. By embracing diversity, promoting inclusion, and implementing the strategies discussed in this chapter, organizations can foster an environment where employees thrive, ideas flourish, and collective success is achieved. Remember, fostering inclusivity is not just the right thing to do; it's a strategic imperative for organizations to attract and retain top talent, foster innovation, and create a positive impact in society. Let us embark on this journey together and make our workplaces more inclusive, equitable, and empowering for all.

Addressing Bias and Promoting Equality

In a world that is becoming increasingly interconnected, it is essential to address bias and promote equality. Bias refers to the prejudice or preconceived notions that individuals hold about certain groups of people based on their backgrounds, characteristics, or beliefs. This bias can manifest in various ways, ranging from subtle microaggressions to overt discrimination. Addressing bias is crucial to ensure a fair and inclusive society where all individuals have an equal opportunity to thrive and contribute to their fullest potential.

Understanding Bias:

Bias, in its various forms, is deeply ingrained in societies around the world. It can arise from personal experiences, cultural influences, media portrayal, or simply the lack of exposure to diverse perspectives. Implicit biases, which are unconscious associations or attitudes towards certain groups, are particularly challenging to address as individuals are often not aware of their own biases. However, it is important to note that bias is not inherently evil but rather a natural human inclination to categorize information quickly. The problem arises when these biases perpetuate stereotypes and lead to discriminatory behavior.

Types of Bias:

Bias can manifest in numerous ways, targeting various aspects of an individual's identity, such as race, gender, sexual orientation, religion, or socioeconomic status. Some common types of bias include:

1. Racial bias: This form of bias is based on the assumption that one race is superior to others. It can lead to systemic discrimination and disparities in education, employment, and criminal justice, among other areas.

2. Gender bias: Bias towards a specific gender often leads to unequal treatment and opportunities. This bias can reinforce gender roles and limit individuals' potential based solely on their gender identity.

3. LGBTQ+ bias: Discrimination against individuals who identify as lesbian, gay, bisexual, transgender, or queer is prevalent in many societies. Such bias can result in exclusion, harassment, and limited legal protections for LGBTQ+ individuals, impeding their ability to live openly and authentically.

4. Religious bias: Often rooted in ignorance and fear, religious bias can lead to discrimination, intolerance, and even violence. Individuals who belong to minority religious groups are particularly vulnerable to biased treatment in various aspects of their lives.

5. Socioeconomic bias: Bias based on an individual's socioeconomic status can perpetuate social inequality. Those who are economically disadvantaged may face limited access to education, healthcare, and basic necessities, further entrenching the cycle of poverty.

Challenging Bias:

Addressing bias is both an individual responsibility and a collective effort involving societal and institutional change. Here are several strategies that can be employed:

1. Education and Awareness: Raising awareness about various forms of bias is a critical first step. Educational institutions, workplaces, and communities must actively provide education and training to challenge stereotypes, promote empathy, and foster cultural understanding.

2. Self-reflection: As individuals, we must engage in self-reflection to become aware of our own biases. By examining our beliefs and attitudes, we can recognize where bias may be influencing our thoughts and actions. This can lead to personal growth and a willingness to confront and overcome prejudice.

3. Fostering Empathy: Empathy is a powerful tool in combating bias. Encouraging open dialogue and honest conversations can help individuals understand the experiences and perspectives of others,

fostering empathy and compassion towards different groups.

4. Dismantling Systems of Inequality: Systemic biases are deeply rooted in societal structures and institutions. It requires a collective effort to challenge and dismantle these systems, pushing for policies that promote equality and fairness.

5. Promoting Diversity and Inclusion: Creating diverse and inclusive spaces is crucial in addressing bias. In workplaces, for example, companies can implement affirmative action programs, equitable hiring practices, and inclusive policies to ensure equal opportunities for all employees.

6. Media Representation: The media plays a significant role in shaping societal perceptions and attitudes. Promoting accurate and inclusive representation in media can challenge stereotypes and biases by providing diverse narratives that reflect the reality of marginalized communities.

7. Engaging in Allyship: Allies, individuals who belong to privileged groups, can play a vital role in addressing bias. By actively supporting and advocating for marginalized communities, allies can use their voice and privilege to create positive change.

Addressing bias and promoting equality requires an ongoing commitment from individuals, communities, and institutions. It necessitates challenging our own biases, engaging in introspection, and actively working towards creating a fairer and more inclusive society. By embedding these principles into our daily lives, we can collectively dismantle structures of oppression and foster genuine equality for all.

Harnessing Diverse Perspectives for Innovation

Innovation has always been the cornerstone of progress and success in any field. From technology to healthcare, education to business, it is the ideas and inventions that emerge from innovative thinking that push boundaries, improve existing systems, and create entirely new opportunities. And at the heart of innovation lies the ability to harness diverse perspectives. By tapping into the power of diverse backgrounds, experiences, and ideas, organizations can foster a culture of creativity, foster collaboration, and drive groundbreaking advancements. In this chapter, we will explore the various aspects of harnessing diverse perspectives for innovation and the tangible benefits that come with it.

Understanding Diversity

Before we delve deeper into the subject of harnessing diverse perspectives, it is essential to clarify what we mean by "diversity." Diversity encompasses more than just gender, race, or ethnicity; it encompasses a broad range of characteristics including but not limited to age, cultural background, socioeconomic status, education, religion, and even personality traits. It is the recognition that every individual is unique, with their own set of experiences and viewpoints, and that embracing this diversity fosters a collective strength that far outweighs the sum of its parts.

Value of Diverse Perspectives

Harnessing diverse perspectives is not just a matter of fulfilling a moral obligation towards inclusivity but also a strategic move for any organization or society aiming to innovate and stay relevant in an increasingly globalized and interconnected world. Diverse perspectives bring fresh ideas, different ways of thinking, and alternative solutions to the table. By inviting minds from various backgrounds to engage in the process, organizations can benefit from a wider range of inputs, insights, and approaches to problem-solving, leading to more effective and creative solutions.

Creative Thinking

One of the key advantages of embracing diverse perspectives is its positive impact on creative thinking. By engaging individuals with varied backgrounds, organizations can foster an environment that stimulates innovation and generates unique and imaginative ideas. When people from different cultures, disciplines, and experiences come together, they bring a wealth of knowledge and alternative ways of approaching challenges. This rich tapestry of perspectives can ignite a synergistic effect, enabling the blending of different ideas and concepts, ultimately resulting in innovative breakthroughs.

One prominent example of harnessing diverse perspectives for creative thinking is the Pixar Animation Studios. Known for their commitment to diversity and inclusion, Pixar encourages collaboration amongst artists, animators, storytellers, and engineers from diverse backgrounds. By fostering an environment where creatives with different skill sets and experiences converge, Pixar has been able to produce groundbreaking animated films, captivating audiences globally. A prime example is the hit movie "Coco," which drew heavily on Mexican cultural traditions and resonated deeply with audiences worldwide. This success would not have been possible without embracing diverse perspectives during its development.

Problem-Solving

Innovation often hinges on finding solutions to complex problems. By harnessing diverse perspectives, organizations can approach problem-solving from multiple angles, thus increasing the likelihood of finding comprehensive and effective solutions. Diverse teams bring together a mix of expertise, experiences, and cognitive styles, enabling them to identify alternative aspects of a problem and devise novel ways to tackle it.

Historically, NASA has prioritized diversity in its pursuit of innovation. In the late 1960s, when NASA sought to overcome the challenge of developing heat shields capable of protecting space shuttles during reentry into the Earth's atmosphere, the agency established a diverse group of engineers and scientists to work on the problem.

By assembling a team that included individuals from various backgrounds and experiences, NASA benefited from a wide range of perspectives on thermal engineering, materials science, and fluid dynamics. This led to the breakthrough development of the advanced heat-resistant tiles that paved the way for successful space missions. The diversity within the team helped them address the technical challenges from multiple angles and eventually achieve their goal.

Inclusive Decision-Making

Harnessing diverse perspectives also enhances the quality and inclusivity of decision-making processes. When multiple viewpoints and backgrounds are considered, it helps guard against unconscious biases, stereotypes, and groupthink that can limit the efficacy of decisions. By actively seeking input from diverse sources, organizations can make more informed choices based on a broader understanding of the potential implications and consequences.

In the political realm, New Zealand provides an illustrative example of inclusive decision-making. In 2018, the country implemented the "Wellbeing Budget," a novel approach to national budgeting that aimed to go beyond traditional economic measurements and encompass wider societal well-being. The development of this groundbreaking budget involved gathering perspectives from a diverse range of stakeholders, including rural and urban communities, indigenous populations, women, youth, ethnic minorities, and people with disabilities. By incorporating the voices and concerns of underrepresented groups, the New Zealand government was able to formulate policies that reflected the country's diverse needs more accurately.

Enhancing Organizational Culture

Harnessing diverse perspectives goes beyond achieving specific innovations; it also significantly impacts the overall culture within an organization. When employees are presented with an opportunity to engage with individuals from diverse backgrounds, it encourages open-mindedness, empathy, and cultural intelligence. These qualities can create a more inclusive work environment where individuals feel valued, respected, and motivated to contribute fully.

Companies like Unilever have recognized and embraced the positive influence of diverse perspectives on organizational culture. Unilever actively encourages the inclusion of diverse voices at all levels, from entry-level employees to senior executives. Their dedication to diversity and inclusivity has resulted in a more vibrant and proactive work environment, fostering collaboration and employee engagement. Research has shown that diverse teams at Unilever have experienced increased innovation, improved problem-solving abilities, and higher profitability due to their inclusive organizational culture.

Challenges in Harnessing Diverse Perspectives

While the benefits of harnessing diverse perspectives are clear, the journey towards creating genuinely inclusive environments is not without its challenges. Overcoming these challenges requires open dialogue, continuous learning, and proactive measures. Some of the common roadblocks and potential solutions to conquer them include:

Unconscious Bias: Unconscious biases, rooted in societal norms and personal experiences, can hinder the equitable consideration of diverse perspectives. Organizations must encourage self-awareness and provide bias training to help individuals recognize and challenge their biases. Additionally, implementing blind recruitment processes or diverse interview panels can mitigate the impact of unconscious biases during hiring decisions.

Lack of Representation: Lack of representation of certain groups can limit the potential contributions from diverse perspectives. Organizations should strive to ensure that decision-making bodies, executive boards, and leadership positions are inclusive and representative of the broader population. Affirmative action policies, mentorship programs, and sponsorship initiatives can be valuable tools in addressing this challenge.

Resistance to Change: Resistance to change is inherent in every organization, and initiatives promoting diversity and inclusivity may face pushback from individuals accustomed to the status quo. Therefore, leaders must communicate the purpose and benefits of embracing diverse perspectives effectively. Providing education and training programs that debunk misconceptions and underline the positive impact of diversity can foster a culture of acceptance and promote change.

Harnessing diverse perspectives for innovation benefits not only individual organizations but also society as a whole. By recognizing and valuing the unique contributions that diverse perspectives offer, organizations can create a culture that fosters innovation, creativity, and inclusivity. A commitment to diversity allows teams to draw from a broader pool of knowledge, experiences, and insights, ultimately leading to more effective problem-solving, enhanced decision-making, and groundbreaking advancements. As we continue to navigate an ever-changing world, embracing diverse perspectives will be crucial in shaping a future that is innovative, equitable, and sustainable.

Chapter 8: Empowering and Delegating Effectively

In today's fast-paced and competitive business environment, effective empowerment and delegation are crucial skills for leaders and managers. In this chapter, we will explore the art of empowering and delegating effectively to achieve better results, foster employee growth, and create a culture of trust and collaboration within organizations. We will delve deep into understanding the concept of empowerment, the benefits it brings, and how leaders can effectively delegate tasks to enhance productivity and employee satisfaction.

Understanding Empowerment

Empowerment is a process that involves giving individuals the authority, responsibility, and autonomy to make decisions and take action within their roles. It involves creating an environment where individuals feel empowered to take ownership of their work, unleash their creativity, and contribute to achieving organizational goals. Empowerment is not about relinquishing control but rather about sharing and distributing power to encourage collaboration and innovation.

The Benefits of Empowerment

1. Improved Employee Engagement: Empowered employees feel valued, trusted, and respected, leading to higher levels of engagement and motivation. When employees have a say in decision-making and their voices are heard, they become more invested in their work and are willing to go the extra mile to deliver exceptional results.

2. Enhanced Problem-Solving: Empowered individuals have the freedom to explore innovative solutions and take calculated risks. By empowering employees to make decisions and solve problems, organizations tap into their collective knowledge and creativity, resulting in more effective and efficient problem-solving.

3. Increased Productivity: When employees are empowered, they feel a sense of ownership towards their work, leading to increased productivity and accountability. By delegating tasks and responsibilities effectively, leaders can distribute workloads evenly and capitalize on each employee's strengths, thus maximizing productivity.

4. Improved Decision-Making: Empowerment enables decision-making at various levels within an organization. When decision-making is decentralized and individuals are empowered, organizations can benefit from diverse perspectives and better

decision outcomes. This approach also helps build a culture of trust, empowering employees to make decisions confidently.

Effective Delegation

Delegation is the process of assigning tasks, responsibilities, and authority to others while still retaining accountability for the outcomes. Effective delegation is essential for successful management and leadership as it enables leaders to focus on higher-level strategic objectives while empowering and developing their team members.

1. Identify Tasks for Delegation: Start by identifying tasks that are suitable for delegation. Tasks that require a lower level of expertise or can be effectively completed by others should be the focus. Delegating routine tasks frees up time for leaders to concentrate on more critical responsibilities.

2. Choose the Right Person: Consider the skills, knowledge, and capabilities of your team members when assigning tasks. Match tasks to individuals who have the appropriate skill set and provide them with the necessary authority and resources to complete the tasks successfully.

3. Communicate Clearly: When delegating, ensure that you communicate expectations, timelines, and desired outcomes clearly.

Lack of clear communication can lead to misunderstandings and mistakes. Discuss the level of autonomy and decision-making authority the individual has, balancing it with any necessary oversight to ensure success.

4. Provide Support: Even when tasks are delegated, it is crucial to provide ongoing support and guidance to the individual. Be available for questions and discussions, offer advice, and provide feedback along the way. It is through this support that individuals can grow and develop their skills.

5. Control and Monitor Progress: While giving autonomy to individuals, the leader should still maintain control and monitor progress. Regularly check in with the individual to ensure they are on track and provide any necessary adjustments or guidance. Open lines of communication foster trust and allow for early identification and resolution of any challenges.

6. Celebrate Success and Learn from Failures: Recognize and celebrate successes when tasks are completed well. Publicly acknowledge and appreciate the efforts of team members, fostering a positive and empowering work culture. On the contrary, when failures occur, focus on learning opportunities rather than placing blame. Encourage individuals to share their experiences and learn from failures to foster a growth mindset.

Empowerment and Delegation in Practice

To illustrate the concepts of empowerment and delegation in practice, let's consider a fictional case study.

Case Study: ABC Tech's Innovation Project

ABC Tech, a leading technology company, is launching an innovation project to develop a groundbreaking product. The project manager, Sarah, understands the importance of empowerment and delegation to drive innovation and harness the full potential of her team.

1. Empowering the Team: Sarah ensures that the project team members are well-informed about the project goals and vision. She encourages open communication, creating a safe space for team members to share their ideas and suggestions. By empowering team members to contribute their expertise, Sarah creates a collaborative environment where innovation thrives.

2. Task Delegation: Sarah analyzes the skills and strengths of each team member and assigns tasks accordingly. She delegates research tasks to the team's skilled researchers, design tasks to the creative members, and project coordination to the detail-oriented individuals. By appropriately delegating tasks, Sarah leverages the strengths of her team, leading to efficient progress and high-quality outcomes.

3. Ongoing Support and Feedback: Sarah regularly checks in with her team members to provide guidance, support, and feedback. She encourages open dialogue, allowing team members to share challenges and seek assistance when necessary. Sarah's approach facilitates the growth and development of her team, leading to a more capable and empowered workforce.

4. Celebrating Success and Learning from Failures: When significant milestones are achieved or innovative ideas are implemented successfully, Sarah celebrates the accomplishments with the entire team. This recognition promotes a positive work environment and motivates individuals to continue contributing their best efforts. Additionally, in the face of setbacks or failures, Sarah fosters a blame-free culture and encourages the team to learn from their experiences, further promoting a growth mindset.

Empowerment and delegation are vital skills for leaders and managers seeking to create successful, collaborative, and innovative organizations. By empowering individuals, organizations can tap into their collective potential, drive engagement, and enhance problem-solving capabilities. Effective delegation enables leaders to focus on strategic objectives, develop their team members, and foster a culture of trust and accountability. Through these practices, leaders can unlock the full potential of their workforce, achieve remarkable results, and pave the way for long-term success.

The Art of Delegation in Leadership

Delegation is an essential skill for effective leadership. It allows leaders to focus on their core responsibilities while empowering team members to contribute and grow within their roles. The art of delegation goes beyond merely assigning tasks; it involves understanding each team member's strengths, building trust, and providing the necessary support for successful outcomes. In this chapter, we will explore the various aspects of delegation in leadership and discuss how it can be mastered to enhance organizational success.

The Benefits of Delegation

Effective delegation is a win-win situation for both leaders and their teams. As a leader, delegating tasks allows you to concentrate on strategic decision-making, fostering innovation, and developing a vision for the organization. By empowering your team members, you not only distribute the workload but also create an environment that encourages collaboration, increases engagement, and nurtures talent.

From a team member's perspective, being delegated tasks provides an opportunity to showcase their abilities, gain new skills, and take ownership of their work. When they are trusted with responsibilities, it boosts their motivation and job satisfaction, ultimately leading to higher productivity and improved performance.

Understanding Team Members' Strengths

Delegating effectively starts with understanding the strengths and capabilities of your team members. Each individual possesses a unique set of skills and experiences, and as a leader, it is crucial to identify and leverage these strengths when assigning tasks. This knowledge enables you to allocate responsibilities that align with each individual's expertise and interests, optimizing their performance and fostering personal growth.

To gain a comprehensive understanding of your team members' strengths, invest time in open communication and active listening. Conduct regular one-on-one meetings, team-building exercises, or even personality assessments to uncover hidden talents and discover opportunities for growth. By doing so, you can delegate tasks that match abilities, resulting in greater satisfaction and increased chances of success.

Building Trust

Successful delegation is built upon a foundation of trust between leaders and their team members. Trust enables open and honest communication, fosters accountability, and establishes a supportive work environment. However, trust is not built overnight; it requires consistency, transparency, and mutual respect.

As a leader, be transparent about your expectations and provide clear guidelines for delegated tasks. Balance control with autonomy, allowing team members the freedom to make decisions while being readily available to provide guidance and support when needed. Encourage open dialogue, where team members feel comfortable expressing their concerns or seeking clarification. By establishing trust, you create an environment that encourages effective delegation and empowers your team.

Effective Communication in Delegation

Communication is paramount in successful delegation. Ambiguity and miscommunication can lead to confusion, inefficiency, and frustration among team members. As a leader, you must ensure clear and concise instructions are provided, conveying your expectations and any relevant information related to the delegated task. When assigning a task, clearly outline its purpose, the desired outcome, timelines, and any constraints or potential challenges. Provide any necessary resources and clarify the decision-making authority delegated to the individual. Be open to questions and actively listen to the concerns or suggestions of team members.

Furthermore, establish regular check-in points to monitor progress and offer constructive feedback. Encourage open communication channels, ensuring team members feel comfortable discussing challenges or seeking guidance when required. Good communication ensures the smooth flow of work, minimizes misunderstandings, and helps build a collaborative environment.

Supporting Delegated Tasks

Effective delegation involves providing the necessary support to ensure delegated tasks are accomplished successfully. Support systems can take various forms, such as mentorship, training, or access to resources and information.

Mentorship plays a crucial role in guiding team members during the delegation process. As a leader, providing mentorship allows you to share your experience and knowledge while empowering individuals to develop their skills. Encourage peer mentorship as well, so team members can learn from and support each other in their delegated tasks.

Training programs and workshops equip team members with the necessary skills and knowledge to excel in their assigned responsibilities. Identify any gaps in their expertise and invest in professional development opportunities to bridge those gaps. By doing so, you not only enhance their abilities but also increase their confidence in tackling delegated tasks.

Additionally, providing access to resources and information ensures team members have the tools they need to succeed. Whether it's technology, data, or specialized assistance, make sure they have what is required to perform their roles effectively.

Overcoming Delegation Challenges

While delegation is an invaluable leadership skill, it can present challenges that need to be navigated. Some common obstacles include the fear of relinquishing control, concerns about competence, and potential employee resistance.

Leaders must remember that effective delegation involves trusting their team members to deliver high-quality work. By clearly defining expectations, providing support, and regular check-ins, leaders can address any concerns about competence and develop trust in their teams.

Employee resistance can arise when delegation is perceived negatively or when past experiences have soured the concept. Transparency, effective communication, and clear understanding of each team member's strengths can help overcome such resistance. Involve team members in the decision-making process and emphasize the benefits of delegation, such as growth opportunities and increased job satisfaction.

Mastering the art of delegation is a critical component of effective leadership. By understanding team members' strengths, building trust, communicating effectively, and providing support, leaders can leverage delegation to empower their teams and achieve organizational success. Delegation is not merely assigning tasks; it is about creating an environment of collaboration, growth, and shared responsibility. When done right, delegation enables leaders to focus on strategic goals while nurturing talent, ultimately driving long-term success.

Developing Trust and Empowerment

In today's rapidly changing and complex world, building trust and empowerment within organizations has become essential for success. Trust lays the foundation for strong relationships, effective teamwork, and open communication. Empowered individuals, on the other hand, drive innovation, take ownership, and foster a culture of collaboration. This chapter delves into the importance of developing trust and empowerment, explores strategies to cultivate them, and highlights real-life examples of how organizations have succeeded in nurturing these invaluable qualities.

The Nature of Trust

Trust, often regarded as the cornerstone of any healthy relationship, is not a concept to be taken lightly. It is a delicate balance that requires continuous effort, transparency, and consistent actions. Trust is fluid; it can be built over time but can quickly erode if not nurtured. Consequently, it is crucial for leaders to foster an environment where trust thrives.

The first step towards building trust is to establish a culture of integrity. Leaders must lead by example, upholding ethical standards and displaying honesty and transparency in their actions. By doing so, they set the tone for the entire organization, encouraging employees to be open and trustworthy in their interactions.

Effective communication plays a pivotal role in developing trust. Open and transparent dialogue establishes a sense of security among team members, minimizing misunderstandings and promoting cooperation. Leaders should actively listen to their employees, respecting their opinions and perspectives. Regular and meaningful feedback is equally important, as it creates an environment where individuals feel valued and supported, reinforcing trust.

In addition, trust is nurtured by sharing information. Leaders should be willing to disclose relevant details about the organization's goals, challenges, and successes, enabling employees to understand the big picture. This sharing of information empowers individuals, increasing their sense of ownership and commitment.

Trust, however, cannot be solely built through actions; it also requires belief in others' capabilities. Leaders must delegate responsibilities, allowing employees to showcase their skills and talents. By demonstrating confidence in their team, leaders foster a sense of trust and empower individuals to take risks and grow professionally.

Empowerment: The Catalyst for Growth

Empowerment is the process of giving individuals the confidence, skills, and authority to make decisions and take ownership of their work. Empowered employees are more engaged, motivated, and willing to go the extra mile to achieve organizational goals.

The first step in nurturing empowerment is to create a culture that values and encourages participation. Employees should feel safe to voice their opinions, challenge the status quo, and contribute to decision-making processes. Leaders must foster a collaborative environment, where diverse perspectives are welcomed, and collective intelligence is leveraged.

To empower individuals, leaders should provide ongoing training and development opportunities. Building the necessary skills and knowledge equips employees with the tools to excel in their roles and take on more significant responsibilities. This investment in professional growth demonstrates trust in their abilities and encourages them to leverage their newfound skills to contribute effectively.

Additionally, leaders should create a supportive environment that empowers individuals to take calculated risks. Encouraging experimentation and accepting failures as learning opportunities cultivates a growth mindset. When employees are empowered to tackle challenges head-on, they become more resilient and adaptable to change.

Delegation is another critical aspect of empowerment. Leaders should assign tasks and responsibilities that stretch individuals' abilities, while providing them with the necessary resources and support to succeed. Delegating authority builds confidence and promotes a sense of ownership, enabling employees to grow into future leaders.

Real-Life Examples

To illustrate the power of trust and empowerment, let us delve into two real-life examples of organizations that have successfully cultivated these qualities.

Example 1: Google

Google, one of the world's most renowned technology companies, has built a culture that thrives on trust and empowerment. Their "20% time policy" allows employees to spend one-fifth of their working hours pursuing passion projects unrelated to their assigned tasks. This policy demonstrates Google's trust in its employees' abilities, encouraging innovation and fostering a sense of empowerment. Many successful Google projects, such as Gmail and Google Earth, were born out of this initiative.

Moreover, Google values transparency and open communication. Regular town halls, where employees can ask questions to the executive team, promote a culture of trust and collaboration. Employees feel that their opinions matter, and this empowerment leads to a highly engaged and motivated workforce.

Example 2: Zappos

Zappos, the online retail giant, has cultivated trust and

empowerment at every level of its organization. One of their unique practices is the "Culture Book," an annual publication where employees share their experiences and perspectives on the company culture. This book serves as a testament to Zappos' commitment to transparency and trust, providing a platform for every employee to have their voice heard.

Zappos also emphasizes the importance of employee development and empowerment. They offer extensive training programs that focus on both professional and personal growth, ensuring that employees can achieve their full potential. By encouraging employees to take ownership of their work and develop new skills, Zappos fosters a culture of empowerment and continuous learning. Developing trust and empowerment is a powerful means of fostering engagement, innovation, and growth within organizations. By establishing a culture of integrity, promoting open communication, and believing in employees' capabilities, leaders can build trust. Empowerment, in turn, is nurtured by creating an environment that values participation, providing ongoing training, encouraging risk-taking, and delegating authority. Real-life examples like Google and Zappos demonstrate the transformative impact that trust and empowerment can have on organizations. These qualities should be consistently fostered, as they are essential for organizations to thrive in our interconnected and dynamic world.

Balancing Control and Autonomy

In the complex landscape of life, we often find ourselves navigating a delicate balance between control and autonomy. These two seemingly opposing forces have a profound impact on our personal growth, relationships, and overall success. Both control and autonomy have their merits, but it is in finding equilibrium between the two that we can truly thrive. In this chapter, we will explore the intricacies of balancing control and autonomy, understanding their interplay and discovering ways to harness them effectively.

Understanding Control:

Control is a concept deeply ingrained in our society. From an early age, we are taught to seek control over our lives, to plan meticulously, and to minimize unpredictability. Control offers a sense of security and certainty, soothing our fears in the face of an uncertain world. We crave control because it affirms our ability to shape our destiny and protects us from vulnerability.

However, excessive control can have unintended consequences. When control becomes rigid, it stifles creativity, limits growth, and hampers our ability to adapt to new situations. An unwavering need for control can breed stress and anxiety, causing us to miss out on new opportunities and experiences. It is essential, therefore, to strike a balance between control and autonomy to foster personal and professional development.

Understanding Autonomy:

On the other side of the spectrum, we have autonomy – the freedom to make choices and decisions independently. Autonomy nurtures individuality, creativity, and self-expression. It enables us to explore uncharted territories, take risks, and discover our true passions. By granting autonomy to others, we empower them to become active participants in their own lives, fostering a sense of ownership and commitment.

However, too much autonomy can be equally detrimental. Without some level of structure and guidance, we may find ourselves aimlessly drifting, unable to make meaningful progress. Excessive autonomy can lead to a lack of accountability, as we may avoid taking responsibility for our actions or fail to consider the impact of our choices on others. Therefore, it is crucial to find a harmonious blend of control and autonomy.

The Interplay of Control and Autonomy:

Balancing control and autonomy is a nuanced dance, requiring a deep exploration of our internal drivers and external influences. At times, we must relinquish control to allow autonomy to flourish, while at others, we need to tighten our grip to harness the potential of control. Understanding the interplay between these forces is key to navigating this delicate equilibrium.

1. Control as the Foundation of Autonomy:

Control serves as the solid foundation upon which autonomy can be built. By developing a strong sense of discipline, organization, and self-awareness, we lay the groundwork for autonomy to thrive. Control allows us to set goals, establish routines, and prioritize our resources effectively, enabling us to pursue our passions and dreams with confidence. It provides structure and direction, making the path to autonomy clearer and more achievable.

2. Empowering Autonomy through Trust:

To strike the right balance, we must learn to trust ourselves and others. Granting autonomy requires faith in our abilities and the belief that we possess the wisdom to make sound decisions. Similarly, it necessitates extending trust to those around us, empowering them to take charge of their lives. When we create an environment of trust, autonomy flourishes while control maintains a supportive role, ensuring that our actions align with our overall values and aspirations.

3. Flexibility and Adaptability:

Finding equilibrium between control and autonomy demands flexibility and adaptability. Life is dynamic, and circumstances change constantly. Embracing a growth mindset and acknowledging that change is inevitable allows us to let go of excessive control and embrace new possibilities.

By being open to different perspectives, embracing uncertainty, and learning from setbacks, we can strike a balance that accommodates both control and autonomy in an ever-evolving world.

4. Collaboration and Communication:

Effective collaboration and communication are fundamental in balancing control and autonomy. By actively engaging with others, we gain valuable insights, broaden our perspectives, and challenge our assumptions.

Collaboration encourages shared decision-making, where both control and autonomy are considered, fostering a healthy exchange of ideas. Through open and honest communication, we can address conflicts, establish boundaries, and negotiate a balance that respects both individual autonomy and collective well-being.

The delicate dance between control and autonomy is an ongoing journey rather than a destination. By cultivating self-awareness, continuously evaluating our actions, and remaining open to growth and change, we can strike a balance that allows us to thrive personally and professionally.

Embracing control as a supportive force and empowering autonomy through trust, flexibility, collaboration, and effective communication, we can navigate life's complexities with grace and purpose. Remember, it is in the harmonious integration of control and autonomy that we find true success and fulfillment.

Monitoring and Supporting Delegated Tasks

Delegation is an essential function in any organization as it enables leaders to distribute tasks and responsibilities among team members, promoting efficiency and growth. However, it is not enough to simply delegate tasks; effective monitoring and support are equally important. In this chapter, we will explore the significance of monitoring and supporting delegated tasks and provide practical strategies for leaders to ensure successful task completion and employee development.

Understanding Delegated Tasks:

Delegated tasks refer to the responsibilities and assignments that are assigned by a leader to a team member. They can range from simple day-to-day activities to complex projects requiring extensive coordination and collaboration. Leaders delegate tasks to optimize resource allocation, foster employee growth, and focus on high-level priorities. By effectively monitoring and supporting these tasks, leaders can ensure that their teams achieve desired outcomes within the specified timeframes.

The Importance of Monitoring:

Monitoring delegated tasks is crucial for several reasons. Firstly, it allows leaders to stay informed about task progress and identify potential roadblocks or issues early on. By being aware of the project's status, leaders can take timely actions, including reallocating resources or revising timelines, to prevent delays or failures. Additionally, monitoring provides leaders with an opportunity to assess the performance of team members and provide constructive feedback that contributes to their professional growth. Regular monitoring cultivates a culture of accountability, where employees have a clear understanding of expectations and their responsibilities in achieving the desired outcomes.

Effective Monitoring Techniques:

To monitor delegated tasks effectively, leaders can employ various techniques. Communication plays a central role in this process. Leaders should establish open lines of communication with team members, ensuring that they feel comfortable approaching them with any questions or concerns. Regular check-ins, either through one-on-one meetings or group discussions, allow leaders to gauge progress, address concerns, and provide support where necessary. It is essential to strike a balance between providing guidance and allowing individuals the freedom to make independent decisions, fostering a sense of ownership and empowerment among team members.

Another crucial aspect of monitoring is setting clear expectations. Leaders should ensure that team members have a comprehensive understanding of their assigned tasks, including specific objectives, expected outcomes, and associated deadlines. By providing clarity, leaders can minimize misunderstandings and promote a shared sense of purpose. Regularly reviewing and reinforcing these expectations reinforces accountability and motivates team members to deliver their best work.

Tracking and documentation are also key components of effective monitoring. Using project management tools and techniques allows leaders to keep track of task progress and deadlines, ensuring that everyone is on the same page. Progress reports, status updates, and shared calendars facilitate transparency and encourage collaboration among team members. Leaders can use these records to identify potential bottlenecks, reallocate resources if necessary, or identify areas of improvement for future projects. Furthermore, documentation provides a valuable reference point to evaluate the efficacy of different strategies deployed during the task execution.

The Role of Support in Task Delegation:

Supporting delegated tasks is equally critical as monitoring. Support encompasses a range of actions designed to facilitate task completion, enhance employee performance, and foster a conducive work environment. By providing the necessary support, leaders can empower team members, boost morale, and inspire confidence, leading to increased productivity and overall success.

Mentoring and Coaching:

One of the most impactful ways leaders can support delegated tasks is through mentoring and coaching. Taking an active interest and investing time in guiding team members not only helps strengthen their skills but also builds trust and enhances collaboration. Leaders can share insights from their own experiences, provide relevant resources, and encourage continuous learning. Mentoring and coaching allow leaders to develop the potential of their team members while fostering loyalty and commitment.

Resource Allocation and Training:

Supporting delegated tasks also involves allocating the right resources to team members. Leaders need to ensure that team members have access to necessary tools, information, and training to successfully complete their assignments. Proactive leaders anticipate the resource requirements and provide the necessary support, preventing delays and frustration. Moreover, providing training opportunities allows team members to develop new skills, enhancing their proficiency and increasing their value to the organization. Leaders should encourage an organizational culture that values continual development and growth.

Facilitating Collaboration:

Leaders can further support delegated tasks by fostering collaboration among team members. Encouraging open communication, sharing knowledge, and promoting diverse perspectives can lead to innovative solutions and higher-quality outcomes. Leaders can facilitate collaboration through team-building exercises, shared workspaces, or even through virtual platforms that enable remote collaboration. By creating a supportive environment that values and encourages teamwork, leaders empower team members to collectively achieve their goals.

Recognition and Rewards:

Acknowledging and recognizing the efforts of team members is a crucial part of supporting delegated tasks. Leaders should celebrate milestones and achievements, providing positive reinforcement and motivation for continued success. Recognition can take various forms, such as public appreciation, rewards, or opportunities for growth and advancement. These gestures not only boost individual confidence but also contribute to overall team morale and job satisfaction.

Monitoring and supporting delegated tasks are fundamental aspects of effective leadership. By prioritizing monitoring, leaders stay informed about task progress, identify issues early on, and provide timely feedback. Effective monitoring techniques, such as clear communication, setting expectations, and documentation, contribute to successful task completion and professional growth. Concurrently, providing support through mentoring, resource allocation, collaboration facilitation, and recognition enhances employee performance and job satisfaction. Combining effective monitoring and support strategies ensure that delegated tasks are accomplished efficiently, empowering teams to thrive in achieving organizational objectives.

www.ingramcontent.com/pod-product-compliance
Lightning Source LLC
Chambersburg PA
CBHW051448050726
47593CB00005B/1973